At Issue

Political Scandals

Other Books in the At Issue Series:

At Issue

Political Scandals

Randy Scherer, Book Editor

GREENHAVEN PRESS
A part of Gale, Cengage Learning

Detroit • New York • San Francisco • New Haven, Conn • Waterville, Maine • London

Christine Nasso, *Publisher*
Elizabeth Des Chenes, *Managing Editor*

© 2008 Greenhaven Press, a part of Gale, Cengage Learning.

For more information, contact:
Greenhaven Press
27500 Drake Rd.
Farmington Hills, MI 48331-3535
Or you can visit our Internet site at gale.cengage.com

LIBRARY OF CONGRESS CATALOGING-IN-PUBLICATION DATA

Political scandals / Randy Scherer, book editor.
    p. cm. -- (At issue)
    Includes bibliographical references and index.
    ISBN-13: 978-0-7377-3763-9 (hardcover)
    ISBN-10: 0-7377-3763-8 (hardcover)
    ISBN-13: 978-0-7377-3764-6 (pbk.)
    ISBN-10: 0-7377-3764-6 (pbk.)
    1. Political corruption--United States--Juvenile literature. 2. United States--Politics
and government--Juvenile literature. I. Scherer, Randy.
    JK2249.P647 2008
    364.1'3230973--dc22
                                  2007037426

Printed in the United States of America
2 3 4 5 6 7 12 11 10 09 08

Contents

Introduction

People around the world have been seemingly buried under headlines, talk shows, and Internet sites, all rushing to expose political scandals. TV personalities point fingers as they discuss Abu Ghraib, Enron, and Mark Foley. Web sites show copies of documents pertaining to Valerie Plame, Jack Abramoff, and the Downing Street Memo. A quick scan through the radio dial reveals the multitude of opinions regarding how these scandals will affect politicians and their political parties. It often seems that political scandals such as the ones named above can be among the major components of modern politics. But just what is a political scandal?

Although there is no single definition, political scandals are generally accepted as widely publicized events that involve the abuse of power or abuse of the public trust by elected or appointed officials. Political scandals can involve politicians or government officials at any level. Actions that are deemed scandalous include plotting to break the law, illegally influencing a governmental decision, accepting illegal campaign donations, and conducting inappropriate sexual relationships.

One aspect all modern political scandals have in common is extensive media coverage. Repeated stories on TV shows, in print media, and on the Internet engage the general public and help create the attention and atmosphere necessary to make what could be an isolated event into a scandal.

Activities are considered scandalous not only because they may be illegal—although some political scandals do not explicitly break the law—but because they threaten the proper democratic functioning of government. For example, the U.S. political landscape is characterized by numerous variations of bribery, in which politicians are given gifts or payments so that they will vote on one or more matters in a way that is favorable to the the person who gives them money. Bribery is considered scandalous because it is the selling of one's vote and a betrayal of the public trust. Numerous politicians have been investigated for bribery, such as William J. Jefferson (Democratic Congressman from Louisiana, investigated for receiving a payment of $100,000 in 2005) and Randy "Duke" Cunningham (Republican Congressman from California, who resigned amid allegations that he took $2.4 million in bribes). Sexual relationships or affairs are also often considered political scandals because they are believed to reveal a politician's moral fiber and judgment. They cast doubt on a politician's character, which is important to the voting public.

A new era of political scandals began in the early twenty-first century, when the Republican Party held the White House and both houses of Congress. British historian Lord Acton once stated that "power corrupts," and as the Republican Party won repeated electoral victories in the late 1990s, by the twenty-first century, the voting public found that single-party rule effectively short-circuited the separation-of-powers concepts in the U.S. Constitution.

Critics point out that with a single party controlling so much of government, there was little incentive for individual members of Congress to exercise oversight over one another because they might cause trouble for members of their own party. Furthermore, the close political ties between the White House and Congress led to little to no checks and balances on the president's power. Finally, lobbyists and corporations directed much of their contributions and gifts towards only those in power—there was no incentive to try to curry favor with Democrats, since they held so little power.

According to Jonathan Turley, Shapiro Professor of Public Interest Law at George Washington University Law School, "The 109th Congress is so bad that it makes you wonder if democracy is a failed experiment. I think that if the Framers went to Capitol Hill today, it would shake their confidence in the system they created. Congress has become an exercise of raw power with no principles—and in that environment corruption has flourished."

As the world continues to see the growth of democratic governments, concerned citizens may question whether politics will ever be free of scandal. The Internet has proven to be a valuable tool in uncovering political scandals. In the short term, the Internet seems to inflame and magnify scandals by getting information to so many people so quickly. However, in democracies, this information is often used in the decision-making process.

Internet-savvy voters around the world have access to seemingly unlimited information that ranges across the spectrum of viewpoints (and of quality), thrusting once secret backroom deals into the public view. U.S. Supreme Court Justice Louis Brandeis wrote "Sunlight is the best of disinfectants" to explain the benefits of openness and transparency. In order to prevent future scandals, organizations such as the Center for Responsive Politics research the interactions between money, politicians, and public policy and publish their findings on the Web. Many other organizations comb through a variety of resources to find and publicize news stories that can lead to the uncovering of what may be both illegal and scandalous behavior.

Thomas Jefferson wrote "[We] should look forward to a time, and that not a distant one, when corruption . . . will have seized the heads of government and be spread by them through the body of the people; when they will purchase the voices of the people and make them pay the price. Human nature is the same on every side of the Atlantic and will be alike influenced by the same causes." Understanding the nature of modern political scandals is crucial to the healthy functioning of a democracy, for history provides the context in which citizens choose future governments.

1

Political Scandals Erode the Public's Trust in the Political System

Sebastian Mallaby

Sebastian Mallaby, a columnist for the Washington Post, *writes about political and economic issues.*

Political scandals have left politicians clamoring to hold one another accountable. When scandals occur, government becomes constrained under efforts to catch others in the wrong, and the overall efficiency of government declines. Although the level of public trust had risen throughout the 1990s and peaked in 2002, issues such as the stagnating Iraq War and various corporate scandals have driven public trust in the political system to extremely low levels. As a result, the public suffers, as government can no longer function properly.

In 1995 Francis Fukuyama came out with a book called *Trust*, in which he argued that a society's capacity for cooperation underpins its prosperity. The same year, Robert Putnam's famous article, "Bowling Alone," lamented that the United States was depleting its stock of precious social capital. The question of trust—in government and also in communities—preoccupied politicians too. *It Takes a Village*, Hillary Rodham Clinton urged in the title of her 1996 book, which became a best seller.

You don't hear much about trust these days. Instead, we want accountability.

Sebastian Mallaby, "The Decline of Trust," *Washington Post*, October 30, 2006, p. A17. Copyright © 2007 the Washington Post. Reprinted with permission.

You see this most viciously in politics. In the mid-term campaigns, nobody has time for trust. The name of the game is to hold opponents accountable by attacking their records— for failings real or imagined. If the Democrats capture one or both chambers [in the November 2006 elections], it will be largely because they promise to hold the president accountable.

This reflects a shift somewhere around 2003 or 2004. In the 1990s, after academics and pundits began talking about trust, the nation did actually become more trusting. The share of Americans saying they trust government "most of the time" or "just about always" rose from 21 percent in 1994 to 56 percent in 2002. Equally, elections became less abrasively focused on accountability. In 2000, according to John Geer of Vanderbilt University, a relatively low 40 percent of the messages in presidential TV spots were negative, down from 47 percent four years earlier.

But some time after the Iraq invasion, these trends reversed. In 2004 the share of Americans saying they trusted government fell to 47 percent, and [in October 2006] a *CBS News-New York Times* poll put it at a rock-bottom 28 percent. Meanwhile Geer's measures show that in the 2004 election negative messages jumped to 50 percent of the total, and he guesses that this year's congressional races are the most negative in history.

Suddenly nobody wanted to trust managers; they wanted to audit them.

Decline in Trust Extends to Corporate America

There's been a similar change in corporate America. In the late 1990s, the new thing for corporate managers was to trust ordinary employees. Company hierarchies were flattened so that people in the middle could demonstrate initiative rather than suffocating under bureaucratic controls. In 1999, the *Harvard Business Review* reported that 30,000 articles on trusting and empowering middle managers had appeared in the business press over the previous four years.

That paradigm ended in 2002 with Enron, WorldCom and dozens of lesser corporate scandals. Suddenly nobody wanted to trust managers; they wanted to audit them. Instead of the era of management empowerment, we entered the era of mandatory online ethics training. Meanwhile private-equity firms are raising record sums to take over companies on the premise that incumbent managers need to be kicked rather than trusted.

The Great Society programs were possible because Americans trusted government in the 1960s.

What to make of this shift? Holding people accountable is a good thing: This season's negative campaigning can be seen (admittedly, with many despicable exceptions) as a healthy reaction to poor congressional performance. Equally, the 2002 scandals justified the Sarbanes-Oxley reforms of corporate governance. There are reasons we hold teachers accountable for failing schools and put travelers through metal detectors.

"Government Is Constrained If Nobody Trusts It"

But trust, when not abused, is nonetheless an asset. Accountants, lawyers and online training sessions impose costs on businesses; it would be cheaper to trust people if that were possible. Likewise, as Marc Hetherington of Vanderbilt University has demonstrated, government is constrained if nobody trusts it. The Great Society programs were possible because Americans trusted government in the 1960s; the creation of the Medicare prescription drug program arguably reflected the peaking of trust in government in 2003. But Bill Clinton's health care reform was thwarted in the low-trust early 1990s, and nobody now trusts government to modernize entitlements. Meanwhile President Bush had enormous foreign policy momentum in 2002–2003 because Americans trusted him. Thanks to the Iraq mess, Americans are now focused on holding Bush accountable, and his options are limited.

There are powerful reasons trust tends to decline and accountability advances. Mobile societies tend to have weak bonds; the Internet makes it easier to hold people accountable and encourages acerbic negativity. And the absence of trust can feed on itself. Leaders function under stifling oversight; this causes them to perform sluggishly, so trust continues to stagnate. But occasionally there is a chance to escape this trap: A shock causes trust to rise, leaders have a chance to lead and there's an opportunity to boost trust still further.

We've recently had a double opportunity. The boom of the 1990s boosted trust in business; the 2001 terrorist attacks boosted trust in government. But CEOs and politicians abused these gifts with scandals and incompetence. Such is the cost of corporate malfeasance and the Iraq war: Precious social capital is destroyed by leaders' avarice and hubris.

2

Political Scandals Will Destroy the Republican Party

Evan Thomas

Evan Thomas is the assistant managing editor of Newsweek.

The Republican Party took control of Congress in 1994 behind Newt Gingrich's strong anti-corruption message encompassed in the Republican "Contract with America." However, years of scandals, corruption, and lack of discipline among Republican congressmen led to Gingrich's resignation as Speaker of the House and ultimately, the loss of control of Congress in 2006. The failure to follow through on promises of better government led voters to lose faith in the Republicans in Congress. Members of Congress have many lessons to learn from the 12 years of Republican congressional rule.

This is how a revolution ends. Not with a bang, or a "thumping," as President George W. Bush called the 2006 Republican defeat at the polls, but with a misdirected phone call and a certain sinking feeling that even the most well-intentioned politicians can grow weary of rectitude and sell out their principles for the right price.

The scene happened almost 10 years ago, when the GOP revolution in the House of Representatives was still fresh, less than three years after Newt Gingrich and his promise of a Republican "Contract with America" had swept aside four decades of Democratic rule in the House. The House in that summer of 1997 was considering passage of its annual transportation bill, routinely a fat pork sausage of legislation, larded with goodies—bridges, tunnels, exit ramps, highway extensions—for individual congressmen to take home to their districts. A band of a dozen true believers from the Class of '94, the congressmen first elected under the Gingrich banner of reform, was meeting in a small room off the floor of the House. They were trying to plot some way to slow down or stop the pork-stuffed bill—to show that the GOP was still true to its campaign promises to cut profligate government spending.

The phone rang. According to one of the congressmen in the room, Joe Scarborough, another congressman—Steve Largent, a former NFL wide receiver and one of the leaders of the group—picked up the receiver and absentmindedly mumbled, "Yeah." At the other end of the line, Largent heard the voice of Elmer G. (Bud) Shuster, the all-powerful, all-beneficent chairman of the House Committee on Transportation and Infrastructure. Shuster, an unabashed practitioner of old-style politics, was notorious in the House for rounding up votes by dispensing highway projects to pliable congressmen. Shuster apparently did not recognize Largent's voice over the phone. The chairman thought he had instead reached a different congressman—who shall remain nameless in this retelling, but who was well known at the time, a stalwart figure who often spoke of "standing up against the Man." Dictating quickly at the other end of the line, Bud Shuster was in a hurry—like Santa Claus on Christmas Eve, he had a lot of deliveries to make. Without pausing for pleasantries, he ticked off five highway projects worth $70 million, the reward to the supposedly high-minded congressman for swallowing his scruples— just this once!—and voting for the 1997 transportation bill. Package delivered, Shuster hung up.

Largent, the ringleader of the plotters, put down the phone and tried not to show his disappointment that one of their fellow do-gooders had apparently given in to temptation. In-

15

stead, as Scarborough recalls the story, Largent sardonically announced, "Well, I don't think [Congressman X] is going to be with us this time." The others in the room dryly laughed, but it was a demoralizing moment, recalls Scarborough. "You get beaten down," says the MSNBC talk-show host. (Contacted by *NEWSWEEK*, Largent, who suffered a stroke this year, said he could not recall the phone call; Shuster could not be reached for comment.) Scarborough told *NEWSWEEK* that it became a "running joke" for members of the Class of '94 to say to each other. "Well, there goes the revolution," every time one of their Contract with America reforms—like imposing term limits on members of Congress—was abandoned by lawmakers intoxicated with power.

Was the fall of the Republican revolution as predictable as the fall of man? Did the GOP revolutionaries, like so many revolutionaries before them, have to become the very thing they had once vowed to change? Gingrich, the former House Speaker, who stepped down in late 1998 before he could be pushed out, blames his successors for taking the low road to disaster. With his fondness for alliterative lists, Gingrich cites four areas where the Republicans fell short or went astray: "Candor, competence, corruption, and consultants." He specifically blames former majority leader Tom DeLay, who effectively replaced Gingrich as the GOP leader in the House from 1999 through 2005. In Gingrich's judgment, DeLay, as well as other Republican leaders, threw away the power of ideas in their narrow focus on self-preservation. "When an institution develops 'the Hammer' as a model, that's not the most intellectual form of leadership," says Gingrich, alluding to DeLay's nickname, earned for his skill at enforcing party loyalty in the handing out of favors to lobbyists and influence peddlers. (DeLay did not respond to *NEWSWEEK's* requests for comment.)

But Gingrich deserves some of the blame himself for providing a grandiose and ultimately weak model of leadership.

The story of the rise and fall of the Republican revolution in the House of Representatives is a timeless story of vanity and hubris—and a cautionary tale for incoming Speaker Nancy Pelosi and the new Democratic leaders, who would like to inaugurate another long period of their party's rule.

The Republican revolution hardly started with Gingrich. The seeds were planted by the GOP's failed but visionary 1964 presidential candidate, Barry Goldwater, and conservative prophet William F. Buckley; the Reagan landslide of 1980 brought the movement to power in the White House and the Senate, which the GOP held until 1986.

The House, however, long seemed a lost cause; it had not been in GOP hands since the first two years of Eisenhower's presidency. It was Gingrich who first saw a way to exploit growing public dissatisfaction with the old Democratic barons of big government in the House, Speaker Thomas P. (Tip) O'Neill of Massachusetts and his successor, Jim Wright of Texas. Gingrich, then an obscure Republican backbencher (O'Neill referred to him as a "stooge," as in the Three Stooges), used a new forum—C-Span—to rail against Democratic corruption. In 1989, somewhat surprisingly, he succeeded in forcing the resignation of Speaker Wright, who was implicated in a scheme to profit off book sales in violation of House rules.

Gingrich had been a bit of a joke even in his own party. The son of a military officer, he seemed to some lawmakers to be a Walter Mitty, a soldier wanna-be who had missed Vietnam (student and family deferments). Gingrich spouted a kind of utopian futurism about the "opportunity society" and handed out tapes so other congressmen could learn, as the accompanying instructions put it, to "talk like Newt." Some congressmen made fun of the tapes. But others listened—and learned. The 1994 congressional campaign was a referendum on big government—Hillary Clinton had launched a massive health-care reform plan that wound up strangled by its own red tape. Gingrich mounted an attack on the "bureaucratic welfare state" that caught the public mood—and shocked the pundits and prognosticators by returning the Republicans with a 26-seat majority in the House.

Suddenly it was Speaker Gingrich. Irrepressible, he launched biting personal attacks on the First Lady, chortling, "We are a happy band of Vikings, who don't mind a fight!" More seriously, he led a campaign that summer to cut federal spending and succeeded in squeezing $50 billion out of the budget before he attacked the hardest nut: Medicare. Gingrich's attempt to trim spending on medical care for the elderly does not seem that extreme—he wanted to restrain the rate of growth from 10 percent a year to 7 percent over seven years. But he immediately ran into a political buzz saw.

Gingrich compared his leadership style to that of Charles de Gaulle, Thomas Edison, and Winston Churchill; he likened his legislative gambits to the battle strategies of the Duke of Wellington and Ulysses S. Grant. "Newt couldn't help himself," recalled Dick Armey, then Gingrich's House majority leader. "He was always just as grand as he could be." At first, President Bill Clinton seemed so diminished by the midterm humiliation that he had to argue that he was "still relevant" at a press conference in the spring of 1995. But by summer, after handling the tragic terror attack on the Murrah Building in Oklahoma City with grace, the president was secretly conferring with an old political consultant, Dick Morris, who was reminding his boss that governing was really a "permanent campaign." At Morris's urging, Clinton launched a demagogic but extremely effective advertising campaign accusing the Republicans of trying to "eliminate" Medicare.

In October '95, Clinton held a press conference at which he charged that the Republicans were cutting health care by $200 billion so they could give the same amount of money back to the wealthy as tax breaks. Joe Scarborough was watching with some fellow freshmen from the Class of '94. "I remember we broke out laughing, saying 'That poor fool,'" Scarborough recalled. The joke was on the Republicans. As the budget battle turned into a stalemate later that fall, the government shut down. Clinton blamed the Republicans, darkly warning that Social Security checks would no longer be mailed out. The president repeatedly outfoxed Gingrich. When Gingrich flew on Air Force One to the funeral of Israeli Prime Minister Yitzhak Rabin, Clinton declined to find and negotiate a budget solution (preferring, instead, to play hearts up front with business tycoon Mort Zuckerman). Gingrich threw a tantrum on their return—and the New York *Daily News* (owned by Zuckerman) ran a front-page cartoon of Gingrich in diapers (which the Democrats made into a poster and, in a mischievous violation of House rules, stuck on the Speaker's chair). Gingrich ultimately caved in and had to plead with his own hardliners to reopen the government.

Rep. Nick Smith charged that "bribes and special deals were offered to convince members to vote yes."

Clinton continued to outflank Gingrich, effectively stealing much of the Republican platform by being tough on crime and welfare and declaring that the era of big government was over. Worn down, Gingrich privately confessed, "I'm not a natural leader. I'm a natural intellectual gadfly." Even after Clinton was consumed by the Monica Lewinsky scandal in 1998, Gingrich was unable to lead; his own troops were already plotting to purge him.

Gingrich's resignation after the 1998 election (the Republicans lost five seats) brought on an interlude that could only be described as comic opera. At the height of the Clinton impeachment proceedings, the new House Speaker-designate, Rep. Robert Livingston of Louisiana, resigned after the publisher of *Hustler* magazine, Larry Flynt, placed an ad in the *Washington Post* offering up to a million dollars for information about sexual indiscretions by DC officials. After a story broke in the press, Livingston admitted to extramarital affairs in a dramatic speech on the floor of the House. Livingston did not run for Speaker and resigned his seat.

Stunned Republicans chose a blandly amiable former high-school wrestling coach, Dennis Hastert, as their next Speaker. But the real power belonged to DeLay, who rose from whip to majority leader in 2003. A former Houston pest exterminator and archfoe of the Environmental Protection Agency, DeLay gave off a cold, hard look that was the polar opposite of sunny Reaganism. He delighted in his "Hammer" nickname. From the beginning of Gingrich's tenure, the GOP's K Street offensive had warned lobbying firms along Washington's K Street corridor that they would be wise to hire Republicans if they wanted access. There was nothing especially new about such a partisan approach to the influence-peddling business. The Republicans had only to look across the aisle to study a past master at shaking the corporate tree—former representative Tony Coelho, the one-time chairman of the Democratic Congressional Campaign Committee. But DeLay brought a new brazenness to the game. Before long, lobbyists could be seen in committee rooms writing legislation. With corporate coziness came the abandonment of fiscal restraint. Committee chairmen now routinely handed out "earmarks," special provisions authorizing spending for members' pet projects. In 1987, President Ronald Reagan vetoed a highway bill because it had 152 earmarks. In 2005, President Bush signed a transportation bill with 6,371 earmarks.

The nadir of the DeLay era may have come in the early-morning hours of Nov. 23, 2003. The Republicans, who had once tried to cut back entitlement programs, were now voting to create a whole new one—a bill to provide prescription-drug benefits for the elderly. Normally, House members have 15 minutes to cast their votes. Instead, DeLay & Co. kept the voting open for three hours—until 6 a.m.—while they persuaded old-fashioned fiscal conservatives to abandon their scruples. The exact nature of the inducements has never been clear, but Rep. Nick Smith charged that "bribes and special deals were offered to convince members to vote yes." (For Smith's vote, the leaders allegedly offered financial and political support for the congressional race of Smith's son.) The House ethics committee, effectively neutered in recent years gave DeLay a wrist-slap reprimand. DeLay accepted the committee's "guidance," adding that he "would never knowingly violate the rules."

The House took on a Darwinian feel. It was every man for himself as staffers and even lawmakers cashed in to become lobbyists. The number of registered lobbyists in Washington nearly doubled, to 37,000, between 2000 and 2006. About half of the 200-odd congressmen who left their seats after 1998 stayed in Washington to become lobbyists or consultants. They would use their privileges as retired congressmen to lobby in the House gym and even on the House floor.

It was perhaps inevitable that the culture of sleaze on Capitol Hill would produce a Jack Abramoff. With his two downtown restaurants and his skybox at the sports arena, Abramoff was a popular host to congressmen and staffers. He was positively gleeful about bilking his clients, ultimately liberating several Indian tribes of $82 million in fees. "I wish those moronic Tiguas were smarter in their political contributions," Abramoff e-mailed Ralph Reed, his friend and the former head of the Christian Coalition. "I'd love us to get our mitts on that moolah!" When Abramoff finally pleaded guilty to fraud, he effectively took DeLay down with him. Several of DeLay's former staffers were caught up in the Abramoff scandal. DeLay was not charged with any wrongdoing, but he was embarrassed by an all-expenses-paid golfing trip to Scotland with Abramoff. Under indictment for campaign-money laundering in Texas in a weak but nagging case brought by a local prosecutor, DeLay gave up his seat in June. (He has pleaded not guilty; the case has not gone to trial.)

Hastert was never able to exercise the same iron control as DeLay. Nor was DeLay's successor as majority leader, John Boehner, able to bring real discipline to fractious House members who looked out primarily for their own political interests. The religious evangelicals became more demanding of the Republican leadership on Capitol Hill, leading to the deeply unpopular spectacle of the Terri Schiavo case. Last year, Senate Majority Leader Bill Frist, eager to court religious conservatives for a possible presidential run, and the House leadership, sensitive to the religious right, intervened to try to keep the patient alive on a feeding tube, a questionable use of federal power, especially for a party that once stood for less government interference.

The GOP's evangelical base was shocked and demoralized this fall when Rep. Mark Foley of Florida was exposed for having sent salacious messages to congressional pages. House leaders blamed each other for not responding to warnings that Foley was a possible sexual predator. In early October, when Hastert was compelled to hold a press conference to announce that he would not step down as Speaker, it was clear that the GOP revolution was in its late Jacobin phase.

Even so, the Republicans might have kept control of Congress had it not been for GOP overreaching on a different front—Iraq. In some ways, the hubris of Gingrich and DeLay was minor compared with the willful risk-taking of President Bush, backed by Vice President Dick Cheney, a former congressman from Wyoming.

History is full of accidents and what-ifs. Cheney was the second-ranking House Republican when he got the call to become secretary of defense in 1989, at the beginning of the George H.W. Bush administration. (Bush's original nominee to become SecDef, former senator John Tower of Texas, was disqualified by allegations that he was a tippling womanizer.) Had Tower not been blocked from taking office, and Cheney not chosen as his Pentagon replacement, Cheney probably would have stayed in the House—and become Speaker when the Republicans won in 1994. "If Cheney had stayed I never would have gone in the leadership," Gingrich told *NEWS-WEEK* last week. Gingrich rated Cheney as a perhaps less imaginative but more politically shrewd lawmaker than himself. Had Cheney stayed in the House and not become a warhawk adviser to both Presidents Bush, history might well have taken a different course. We will never know. But we do know this: Democrats who, in the glow of victory, now say that none of this could happen to them ignore the story of the last dozen years at their peril.

3

Political Scandals Will Not Destroy the Republican Party

William Kristol

William Kristol is the editor of the Weekly Standard *and the chairman of the Project for the New American Century.*

Despite the fact that the Republican Party of 2005 was embroiled in a variety of political scandals, voters care more about issues than these individuals and their troubles. Although the media may claim that electoral victories have to do with opponents' scandals, in reality elections hang on ideological differences, not individual wrongdoings. The public has a much greater concern in policy, not the private lives of politicians. As of 2005, the American public favors many conservative positions, and the Republicans will pull through the current scandals because of this.

[I
n October 2005, the *Weekly Standard*] suggested . . . that a beleaguered President Bush was "poised to rebound by getting back to basics, and getting back to a core, winning agenda." Sure enough, *USA Today* reported a week later that Bush's poll ratings had rebounded to 45 percent approval/50 percent disapproval from a low earlier in the month of 40 percent approval/58 percent disapproval.

I know, I know. Correlation is not causation. It is a fallacy to claim *post hoc ergo propter hoc* [Latin, "after this therefore because of this"]. And so forth. The *Weekly Standard* won't try to take credit for the president's 5-point bounce. Still, it is

William Kristol, "Policy Trumps Scandal," *Weekly Standard* vol. 11, no. 4, October 10, 2005. Reproduced by permission.

startling that during a period in which headlines featured the [suspicious and potentially illegal] stock sale of GOP Senate leader Bill Frist, the indictment of GOP House leader Tom DeLay, the CIA-leak testimony of Judith Miller, and the arrest by the FBI of Jack Abramoff-Grover Norquist associate and White House official David Safavian, the president seems to have done fine. What lessons are to be drawn from that?

Not, we hasten to add, that sleaze is good. It isn't. Not that there aren't real problems with the ethics and the policies of some of those associated with the Republican majorities on the Hill or the Bush administration. There are. And not that Republicans and conservatives shouldn't be worried about the reality, and the perception, of a "culture of corruption." They should be.

Policy matters most.

The Public Cares About More Than Scandals

But the poll numbers do remind us that while "corruption" matters, it doesn't necessarily trump all. The media love scandal stories, but citizens put them in perspective. The citizenry tends to reserve judgment on charges and accusations about which they don't yet know all or even most of the facts. Sensible people don't leap to generalize from a few cases about a whole administration or an entire political party. And they tend to care more about substantive policies and real-world results than they do about alleged sleaze or even corruption. As John J. Dilulio Jr. put it (in a somewhat different context) in his contribution to our tenth anniversary symposium, "policy matters most."

What about the 1994 Republican electoral victory? Wasn't that campaign, which resulted in the biggest electoral swing in a generation, about the corruption of the Democratic Congress? Actually, no. Jim Wright and Tony Coelho were forced to resign in 1989—and had been long replaced and forgotten by 1994. The House banking scandal broke in 1991, and was an issue in the 1992 elections—but not 1994.

In fact, the 1994 campaign was about policy—and ideology. It was about replacing big government liberalism with a conservatism reformist in its policies and traditional in its values. It was about the failed Clinton health care plan, the tax hikes, and gun control measures passed by the Democratic Congress over GOP opposition, about Clinton/Democratic moments like gays in the military and [controversial statements made by then-U.S. surgeon general] Joycelyn Elders on sex and Lani Guinier on race [leading up to her failed nomination for assistant attorney general for civil rights], about fecklessness abroad in Somalia and Haiti. The 1994 campaign was the most ideological in the last two decades. The next most ideological, in fact, was probably 2004.

Republicans Win on the Issues

And in both of these campaigns Republicans did well. Guess what? There is a natural more-or-less conservative majority in the country for economic growth/strength abroad/socially conservative policies, and, conversely, there is quite a lot of hostility to liberal activist judges, high taxes, and American weakness. Obviously, elected officials should pursue the policies they think right, regardless of possible electoral implications in the future—and, even more obviously, regardless of week-to-week poll results. But insofar as electoral considerations can't help but intrude, the president and Republicans should take heart. Bush rebounded, despite the "culture of corruption" story line being pushed by the Democrats and the media, over the last ten days [early October 2005]. He did so because of the John Roberts debate and victory, because of sound and energetic leadership of the executive branch vis-a-vis hurricane Rita, and in a climate of repeated expressions of determination to stay the course in Iraq, as well as because of some openness to GOP congressional calls for spending restraint and for extending the tax cuts.

The next three months will be key for Iraq, important for budget and tax policy, and crucial to the future of constitutional law. If the Bush administration gets those right and doesn't lose its nerve, all the rest shouldn't matter too much.

4

Political Scandals Do Not Sway Voters

David Weigel

David Weigel is an associate editor of Reason.

Sensational scandals such as the Jack Abramoff scandal in 2006 failed to capture the public's imagination. Washington insiders can become enraptured in similarly specific scandals, but voters take in the big picture. Politicians who ran on the corruption of their opponents typically lost. The voting public puts scandals in context and is far more concerned with other issues that affect the nation as a whole.

[In early 2006], Washington pundits could agree on one thing: The Jack Abramoff [lobbying and fraud] scandal was going to shake the city to its foundations. *New York Times* columnist Frank Rich opined that "Watergate itself increasingly looks like a relatively contained epidemic of corruption" next to l'affaire de Jack. Awarding a journalism prize to *Washington Post* investigative reporter Susan Schmidt, *Bloomberg's* Washington managing editor, Al Hunt, said "the Abramoff affair may be the biggest and sleaziest scandal since Watergate." Rumors swirled that dozens of representatives and senators would be dodging indictments. House Speaker Dennis Hastert? Senate Minority Leader Harry Reid? President [George W.] Bush? No one was safe.

But they're all safe now. The Abramoff scandal has largely been a bust—a DC version of the 2005 Red Sox or *Lady in*

David Weigel, "They Don't Know Jack: The Abramoff Scandal Thrills Washington but Bores Voters," *Reason*, vol. 38, October 2006, pp. 12–15. Copyright 2006 by Reason Foundation, 3415 S. Sepulveda Blvd., Suite 400, Los Angeles, CA 90034, www.reason .com. Reproduced by permission.

the Water (a much-hyped movie that flopped in 2006). The dozens of ruined careers have been pared to four: failed Georgia lieutenant governor candidate Ralph Reed, former Majority Leader Tom DeLay (R-Texas), Rep. Bob Ney (R-Ohio), and, pending the next election's results, and Sen. Conrad Burns (R-Mont.). The Democrats, who spent months talking about a Republican "culture of corruption," dialed down that message and pivoted to simpler, worn-in issues like the minimum wage.

In April [2006] the *Weekly Standard*'s Matthew Continetti published *The K Street Gang*, a wide-ranging history of Abramoff and the lobbying culture in GOP-dominated Washington. *Gang* was promoted to millions of readers and viewers on the *Daily Show*, in the *Washington Post*, in *Reason*. Doubleday printed an initial run of 50,000 copies. According to Nielsen Bookscan, around 47,000 of them never left the bookstore shelves. The word went out to publishers and agents: Don't buy any Abramoff books.

Why did the fedora-sporting lobbyist who was going to bring down the GOP become such a dim star in the 2006 election campaigns? Because Washingtonians failed to grasp how poorly the "corruption" issue was playing beyond their borders, and looked past what voters really were angry about.

Americans Already Believed Congress Was Corrupt

Americans never caught on to the details of the Abramoff scandal and never indicated that they cared about it. One reason: They didn't need convincing that Congress was crooked. A January [2006] Gallup poll found 49 percent of the public agreed that "most members of Congress are corrupt." Gallup took the survey again in May, after Abramoff stories had led nightly newscasts and eloped with the A-I pages of Americans' newspapers. The new "pox on all their houses" number: 47 percent.

"This was a kind of 'I've been in Washington too long' moment," says Michael Crowley, a senior editor at the *New Republic* who covered the Abramoff scandal. "I don't think I appreciated the degree to which that was the sentiment. 'Surprise, surprise! They're all corrupt.'"

Americans didn't need convincing that Congress was crooked.

Americans were bored. They were also, in all probability, confused. When the GOP took over Congress in 1995, the well-connected Abramoff started lobbying Congress to loosen regulations on Indian tribes' casino operations. Abramoff and his allies proceeded to bilk the tribes and use the profits to buy trips for congressmen and put their hooks into other, riskier businesses, such as casino cruises off the coast of Florida. The latter venture connected Abramoff's team with an Agatha Christie-ready cast of criminals; a circus of bad deals and murders finally unraveled the game. It isn't a dull story, but it was too thorny and obscure to connect with voters.

Democrats Can't Make Scandals Stick

The Democrats had planned to run on the Abramoff scandal's fumes. In a January memo, when the lobbyist was shuttling from courtroom to courtroom and making his guilty pleas, [Democratic] Senate Minority Leader Harry Reid (or one of his flacks) wrote a memo mulling a national anti-Jack campaign. The document overran with glee about a scandal that "strike[s] at the heart of the Republican political machine that stretches from Congress to K Street, to the White House and back."

"I don't think anyone thought millions and millions of Americans would march to polls to vote against Jack Abramoff," says Ed Kilgore, vice president for policy at the

Democratic Leadership Council. "But it was useful for opinion leaders and elites. It was part of a larger narrative of this Republican Congress that had been around too long and gotten corrupt and incompetent."

The Democrats' "culture of corruption" blitz was stopped cold by two Donkey Party candidates. One was Francine Busby, a school board member and Democratic candidate for Congress in California's 50th District. The previous steward of the San Diego and Orange County-based seat had been Republican Rep. Randy "Duke" Cunningham, who in March had tearfully pleaded guilty to taking $2.4 million in bribes from defense contractors. Cunningham went to jail, and Busby, his vanquished 2004 opponent, ran again for the seat. She faced a former Republican congressman and current energy lobbyist named Brian Bilbray.

It was a perfect test case for Democrats to shower voters with ads, mail, and speeches about how corrupt the Abramoff-tainted GOP was, and how a lobbyist like Bilbray couldn't fix it.

Voters Are Interested in Other Issues

But as a political issue, corruption collapsed at the starting line. Bilbray ran on walling off the Mexican border and denying amnesty to migrant workers. His slogan: "Proven tough on illegal immigration." The immigration issue was overshadowing the corruption jibes even before Busby made a fatal gaffe and told a group of Spanish-speaking workers that they didn't "need papers for voting." Five days later, Bilbray won the election.

Democrats were flummoxed. Their polls showed voters were angry at Congress. But they weren't angry about the scandals. They were angry at Congress's perceived softness on illegal immigration, and angry at legislators ramming pork projects into bills via "earmarks" (which Bilbray denounced, although once elected he voted down new restrictions on earmarking). If voters in an election for a seat opened up by a bribery scandal didn't care about corruption, where, exactly, would the issue play?

If Busby made the narrative dubious, Rep. Bill Jefferson (D-La.) obliterated it altogether.

As the year ran on and the Abramoff scandal started to drift out of the spotlight, the FBI revealed that it had built a solid bribery case against the congressman from New Orleans, linking him to a Nigerian high-tech firm and excavating $90,000 in cash disguised as lasagna in his freezer. It became much harder to frame the Democrats as the party of clean politics.

"I think Jefferson [dealt] a pretty severe blow to the viability of the [corruption] message," The *New Republic*'s Crowley says. "It's not at all comparable to the Abramoff scandal, which was basically a vast conspiracy, but it's hard to make that connection to voters. And 'cash in the freezer' is a pretty handy and quick comeback."

What happened in May was even more important. After the FBI raided Jefferson's congressional office, the Republican House leaders pounced to defend him. Rep. John Boehner, the chain-smoking Ohioan who had replaced Tom DeLay as majority leader, condemned the FBI for its "invasion of the legislative branch" House Speaker Dennis Hastert locked arms with House Minority Leader Nancy Pelosi to demand that Jefferson's files be returned or locked away.

That response hurt Congress' image as much as all of the year's scandals. Voters can be enticed back to the polls if the worst thing their congressman is accused of is working with lobbyists or taking pricey trips. But the idea of politicians circling the wagons to defend a colleague from a justified investigation made them furious. An ABC News poll taken after the raid showed 86 percent of Americans backing FBI searches of congressional offices, nearly double the number who worried about their congressman being corrupt.

Journalists on the Abramoff beat warn that more indictments could come down. The Democrats, who need an Uzi full of silver bullets if they're to take over Congress, are holding out hope that the scandal isn't over. But it is. The "corrupt lobbyist buys Washington" narrative just wasn't compelling. Voters are spitting mad at Washington: They're mad about spending, the Iraq war, the self-parodying immigration deadlock, and the idea that people in DC deserve special protection from the law.

5

Political Scandals Positively Affect Voter Turnout

Rod Liddle

Rod Liddle is a British journalist who has worked for a variety of British news outlets, including the BBC and the Spectator.

Although politicians and insiders claim that the public is not interested in scandals, elections that have hinged on corruption have had larger voter turnouts. Politicians claim that voter turnout has declined in recent years because of the relentless coverage of scandals, but voters have stopped coming to the polls because the parties have become so similar. When there is something to vote for or against—which is easy to recognize in a scandal—voters do show up to vote. If more of the truly scandalous actions of government were widely known, the public would become even more involved in the political process.

Why are we so disillusioned with, or uninterested in, our politicians at the moment [January 2003]? The current thesis—propagated, in the main, by politicians themselves, and swallowed whole by journalists who should know a lot better—is that they are traduced and misrepresented by a vindictive and irresponsible media.

Before he was promoted to the rank of Education Secretary, Charles Clarke was the unelected and many would say imposed chairman of the Labour party, who spent much of his time attempting to convince broadcasters and print journalists that the dwindling electoral turnout was down to them, i.e., the messengers. Journalists spend too much time on 'process' rather than 'policy', the strange, bat-eared former public schoolboy avowed; hence the 'public'—that lumpen, undifferentiated mass—became alienated and estranged from and, indeed, bored by the entire business. 'Process', it later transpired, meant stuff like [member of Parliament] Stephen Byers and others telling lies all over the place.

Clarke is not alone in promulgating this absurd argument. In fact, it has become almost an article of faith among the political classes of Left and Right, a mantra to be recited every time there is an election and the turnout slips, inevitably, below 40 per cent: there's nothing wrong with how we act or what we do—it's how we're represented. There were echoes of this self-serving theory of victimization in Estelle Morris's weak valedictory interview on *Newsnight*. And, more clearly still, in that revelatory cri de coeur from [in 2003, the Prime Minister] Tony Blair to the assembled hacks at the end of the Cherie Booth/Peter Foster [a scandal involving Cherie Booth, Tony Blaire's wife, and a convicted conman Peter Foster] imbroglio: 'You've had your pound of flesh.' . . .

Here we are, they cry, citizens who wish for nothing more than to be of service to the public, and you pursue us as if we were criminals. Really, guys, it's just not fair. And it is undermining faith in the political system.

It is precisely because there is so little for the public to get a grip on in terms of policy issues—the lack of an ideological divide—that we voters sometimes fail to see the point of turning up at the polling booth.

The extent to which this notion has taken root beyond [London postal district] SW1 is surprising. The [British Broadcasting Corporation] BBC, for example, recently [as of January 2003] carried out a review of its political programmes and decided, among other things, that there was too much cynicism kicking around and that more attention should be given to those neglected 'policy' issues, rather than to the stuff of 'Westminster gossip' (i.e., people telling lies to the electorate).

It is a theory, though, which is very easily disproved.

Scandals Energize Elections

For a start, at every election where, locally, some scandal, pursued with avidity by the media, has occurred, the turnout has gone up, not down. Voters become energized by the possibility of booting out a miscreant, and turn up in their droves to do so.

Secondly, it is precisely because there is so little for the public to get a grip on in terms of policy issues—the lack of an ideological divide—that we voters sometimes fail to see the point of turning up at the polling booth. We would like to be given the choice between conflicting analyses of society but, instead, we are invited to be the judges in a rather ghastly beauty contest.

Look what happened when the [British National Party] BNP stood for election in Burnley, Blackburn and Oldham: more people voted. They had something tangible to vote against. And, indeed, for.

So, this might explain why the turnout overall has dropped over the last ten years, but it doesn't explain why politicians themselves are now lower in the public esteem than even lawyers.

Scandalous Arguments in Parliament

Two instances from last week's Prime Minister's Questions provide a clue, however. The first was a classic of its kind, so let me share it with you, in case you missed it.

Charles Hendry is the Conservative [Minister of Parliament] MP for Wealden, in Kent and Sussex. His constituents suffered badly in the recent floods and there was no doubt, in

Mr Hendry's mind, as to who was responsible for this. Not God, or even global warming, but Tony Blair, 'Does he understand why people in Wealden feel betrayed by the Prime Minister?' he cried, having earlier suggested that Mr Blair had promised to stop the floods, somehow.

You can imagine them, can't you, the benighted people of Uckfield and Buxted, wading about in their galoshes, murmuring to each other, 'Gaw, look at this rain. It's worse than ever. I blame that ponce, Tony Blair. Tell you the truth, I feel bloody well betrayed'. . .

Of course, the appropriate response to such a whacko allegation from an opposition MP is simply this: 'The Honourable Member for Wealden is an imbecile. Next question, please.'

Normal people, when asked important questions, realise that they are important and attempt an answer.

I accept that this contravenes parliamentary etiquette, so something less foulmouthed but equally dismissive would suffice, I suppose. But that's not what happened. That's not what the PM said. What actually happened was that the Prime Minister leaned forward and proudly announced that since New Labour had taken office, '5,000 homes which would have been flooded have not been.'

Now, I would defy any member of the public who witnessed this bizarre exchange to come to any conclusion other than that both Mr Hendry and Mr Blair are mentally ill. It is an exchange so utterly removed, so totally divorced, from the real world that it could quite easily pass as satire. But it was not satire; there was no irony.

Nobody believes Tony Blair can stop the floods. Nobody believes it is his fault that flooding has occurred. You can knock up a few flood-prevention schemes here and there but it won't stop the rain, or, on exceptional occasions, the flooding.

And nor does anybody believe the PM's entirely typical assertion that New Labour has stopped the flooding for—what was it again?—'5,000 homes'. Why did he engage in such a flagrantly stupid argument? Why? Because that's how politics is just now: a succession of flagrantly stupid arguments and dishonest statistics. This is what you get when principle and philosophical disagreement are removed from the parliamentary equation.

Avoiding Questions Is Scandalous, Too

Later, and more seriously, we were able to observe another example of why we have all become so disaffected with politics. The Prime Minister was asked a sensible, very clear, question by Charles Kennedy about the likelihood of war being waged against Iraq. What happens if the UN inspectors find nothing but the US still wants to invade, was the gist. What will Britain do then?

I cannot, offhand, think of a more salient or important question to be asked of the Prime Minister. But it is a measure, perhaps, of our chronic disillusion that nobody was very shocked or surprised that Blair didn't even remotely attempt to answer it. What would it take for our troops to be committed to war was the essence of the question. Obfuscation and side-stepping was the answer.

Normal people, when asked important questions, realise that they are important and attempt an answer, or perhaps confess that they do not know. Normal people, hearing Blair's strange, evasive, circumlocutions on the issue of Iraq, should feel deeply aggrieved and—yes, Mr Hendry, this time the term is appropriate—betrayed.

6

Women Have Fewer Sex Scandals Than Men

Steve Chapman

Steve Chapman is a columnist and editor for the Chicago Tribune.

Although many male politicians have had a wide variety of sex scandals, almost no women have. There are four times as many women in Congress today as there were 30 years ago, yet there has not been a single sex scandal involving a female politician in the United States. Women have been involved in other scandals, such as bribery and other abuses of power. Social and physiological factors may account for the lack of female sex scandals. As the representation of women in government better reflects the general society, we may see fewer and fewer sex scandals.

Political sex scandals come in all varieties. Some involve Democrats, and some implicate Republicans. Though most feature consenting adults, the exploitation of minors is not unknown. Neither heterosexuals nor homosexuals are immune. Virtually all these episodes, however, have one thing in common: The politician is a man.

The list of male officeholders who have gotten tangled in embarrassing shenanigans is long and colorful, including Rep. Wilbur Mills (D.-Ark.), who consorted with a stripper known as the "Argentine Firecracker," Sen. Bob Packwood (R.-Ore.), who had a habit of kissing women without their consent, Gov. Arnold Schwarzenegger (R.), a serial groper, and Bill Clinton.

Steve Chapman, "Why Don't Women Have Sex Scandals?" *Human Events*, October 9, 2006. Copyright 2006 Human Events Inc. Reproduced by permission.

House Speaker Dennis Hastert (R.-Ill.), who has been accused of mishandling the Mark Foley case, should have known the perils of unconstrained libidos on Capitol Hill. He got his job only after predecessor Bob Livingston (R.-La.) was revealed to have cheated on his wife.

And one thing any speaker should know is that the next sex scandal is a matter of when, not if. I could fill up the rest of this column with the exploits of congressmen who had trouble keeping their pants on.

Are Sex Scandals A Men's Only Club?

But not congresswomen. I tried to find examples of female politicians ensnared in such sordid doings, and came up with only one—in Taiwan. Over the last 30 years, the number of women in Congress has quadrupled, and they now make up one of every six members. Though they do their share of the legislative work, they fall terribly short when it comes to bedroom escapades.

On average, males end up with twice as many cells in the area of the brain for sexual pursuit.

The closest recent thing [as of October 2006] I could come to a woman politician involved in a sex scandal is Jeanine Pirro, whose campaign for New York attorney general is in trouble because she reportedly had her husband's phone bugged. What's the sex angle? She suspected he was having an affair.

It used to be assumed that once women gained a measure of parity in elective office, they would fall prey to the same temptations as men—bribery, dirty campaign tactics, delusions of grandeur and jumping into bed with hot subordinates. While they may compete on the first three, they have failed to break the male monopoly on illicit liaisons.

A Biological Explanation for Sex Scandals

Why is that? For an answer, I called Louann Brizendine, a neuropsychiatrist at the University of California, San Francisco, and author of the new book *The Female Brain*, which addresses the biological differences between the minds of men and women. She sounds completely unsurprised that male politicians are far more prone to tripping over their zippers.

"On average, males end up with twice as many cells in the area of the brain for sexual pursuit," she says. Females, her research indicates, devote less of their brain space to getting into other people's pants, and spend far less time fantasizing about sex. It's no accident that guys account for the vast majority of pornography consumers and strip-joint patrons.

Females also have plenty of interest in sex, but because of different brain structure and different hormones, they generally use different strategies to get it—inviting attention by enhancing their appearance, for example, instead of relentlessly hitting on potential partners. Says Brizendine, "It's the pursuit that gets males in trouble."

That's easy to see. Males find the same hormones that make them frisky can also lead them into sleazy or criminal behavior. Married men, Brizendine says, are nearly twice as likely to have affairs as married women, and males account for some 90% of pedophiles in prison.

Guys also seem more inclined to use positions of authority to gain sexual favors, which can be a fatal temptation for some congressmen. It's true that we occasionally hear lurid tales of female schoolteachers seducing underage boys. "Those become major stories because they're so rare," says Brizendine.

What If Congress Were Not Dominated by Men?

The obvious conclusion is that any organization that is predominantly male is doomed to be embarrassed periodically by some lunkheaded horndog. But no law says Congress has to be predominantly male. Nowadays, Brizendine points out, women make up a majority of college graduates and outnumber men in law schools and most other graduate programs.

She sees nothing in the female psyche that would steer them away from elective office. Instead of the current male domination of Congress, she says, "I wouldn't be surprised to see 50-50 or even 60-40 female-to-male someday."

The comic strip "Sylvia" once gave a synopsis of a world without men: "No crime and lots of happy, fat women." But anyone who relishes a good congressional sex scandal would be very bored.

7

Efforts to Prevent Scandals Have Been Ineffective

Charlie Cray

Charlie Cray is a contributing editor to Multinational Monitor *and the director of the Center for Corporate Policy.*

Opportunities for ethics reform rarely present themselves, yet Congress has chosen to let the current chance to clean up corruption slip by. Amid numerous scandals involving lobbyists, campaign finance, bribery, and other abuses of power, members of Congress often talked tough, but did not follow their words with action. Republicans were accused in the majority of scandals, but they also had the majority in both Houses of Congress, and they used this power to block efforts at reform. Eventually, both parties were dragged into the mess, as they passed weak, meaningless reform efforts and allegations against Democrats surfaced as well.

[Former senator] Tom DeLay finally resigned, [lobbyist] Jack Abramoff will soon be doing time, and more indictments are being filed against an ever-growing list of K Street [area in Washington DC known for lobbyists, advocacy groups and think tanks] fixers, Members of Congress and corrupt executive branch employees, fueling public perception that Washington's "culture of corruption" is out of control. Yet all the skeletons and scandals have failed to galvanize enough public outrage to force Congress to pass even modest ethics and lobby reform legislation.

Charlie Cray, "Combating the Culture of Corruption. Or Not," *Multinational Monitor* vol. 27, no. 3 May–June 2006. www.multinationalmonitor.org/mm2006/052006/cray.html. Copyright © 2006 Essential Information, Inc. Reproduced by permission.

Perhaps it's no surprise that Congress dragged its feet until it was too late. Both parties have been accused by ethics watchdogs and reformers of endlessly dickering over the details of key legislation, while using the relatively obscure drafting process to quietly strip out the toughest provisions. Almost from the start, few expected a law would pass that had real teeth. But if the fall of Abramoff, DeLay, [Randy] Cunningham and others is not enough to cause real change, the question is, what will it take?

"The opportunities to enact basic government integrity reforms are cyclical in nature," says Fred Wertheimer of Democracy 21, one of a handful of public interest groups that have closely monitored the lobby reform debate. "They come when problems and scandals arise, as they have now."

Basic reform, however, appears nowhere on the horizon.

Almost everyone working to clean up congressional corruption—in both legal and illegal manifestations—agrees that the key reform is public financing of elections. However, with that proposal deemed unrealistic in the current Congress, government reform groups have coalesced around a reform agenda that seems modest in light of current scandals. And even that set of proposals is going nowhere.

A Simple Plan for Reform

The persistent public interest watchdogs joined together in proposing a six-point plan for lobbying reform back in January [2006]. The original proposals included:

- Cutting lawmaker-lobbyist financial ties;

- Banning corporate-funded air travel;

- Banning gifts to members of Congress and their staff;

- Slowing the revolving door by which individuals shuttle between government and corporate/lobbyist positions;

- Strengthening lobby disclosure requirements; and

- Establishing an independent agency to oversee and enforce ethics rules and lobbying laws.

None of these proposals would survive the legislative chopping blocks, though their supporters believed they were able to amass overwhelming evidence to back each of them.

The proposal to cut ties between Members of Congress and lobbyists seemed among the most likely to gain traction. The public interest groups proposed capping election contributions to candidates from lobbyists and lobby firm PACs (political action committees); prohibiting lobbyists from soliciting, arranging for or delivering contributions to or serving in an official capacity on candidate committees and leadership PACs; prohibiting lobbyists from arranging contributions to foundations and other entities established or controlled by members of Congress; and banning lobbyists and their organizations from underwriting events to "honor" members of Congress and political parties.

There are now 35,000 lobbyists in Washington—68 for every member of Congress. Business is plowing ever more money into lobbying. According to the Center for Responsive Politics, the top 10 lobbying firms reported a combined lobbying income of less than $2 million in 1989, a figure that exploded to $200 million for the top 10 lobbying firms in 2002. No one thinks that corporate lobbyists' effectiveness rests primarily on their ability to make good arguments; rather, key to their power and access is the money they donate directly to Members of Congress, and the money they are able to raise on their behalf.

Jack Abramoff may have played the influence-peddling game to an extreme by engaging in outright bribery, but most of what he did—arranging for and hosting fundraisers, underwriting foreign travel junkets, picking up the tab at his restaurant and extending invitations to his skybox, offering lobbying jobs to congressional staff, laundering money through a charity to pay lobbyists, setting up Astroturf lobbying operations and employing politicians' spouses—are routine tools of the trade in Washington. Abramoff just used a lot more of them, more aggressively and carelessly, than most lobbyists do.

Limiting Lobbyists Can Limit Scandals

The public interest groups proposed a variety of provisions that directly addressed many of these abusive techniques. Many were contained in the reform bills introduced soon after Abramoff took his perp walk. Some were introduced before, including the Lobbying and Ethics Reform Act, introduced by Senator Russell Feingold, D-Wisconsin, in July 2005. None are on track to be enacted into law.

One example is a proposal to ban corporate-funded air travel, perhaps the easiest and mildest reform proposed. Public Citizen's Congress Watch reports that lawmakers received $17.6 million in free travel from private companies and lobbying groups between 2000 and mid-2005. Although Jack Abramoff's famous trips to the Marianas and Scotland receive the most media attention, other lobbyists spent even more, including Richard Kessler, who controlled private companies and organizations that provided Members of Congress with more than $1 million in free travel during the period. By funneling travel money through the Ripon Society and other groups, Kessler apparently made it possible for lawmakers to take free trips to Europe and various resorts without technically being in violation of ethics rules.

Congress has become a way station to wealth . . . Lobbying has become the top career choice for departing Members.

As the Abramoff scandal broke open, House Speaker Dennis Hastert said he would push for a ban on all outside support for congressional travel (a proposal public interest groups said was too broad, because it would block legitimate educational travel for Members of Congress). Hastert's announcement sent House and Senate Democrats scrambling to draft their own proposal—until Hastert kick-started the issue, no Democrat was willing to discuss a ban on privately sponsored travel. The Democratic bills would have allowed only non-profit groups with no ties to lobbyists to pay for privately sponsored travel—and only if lobbyists were not allowed to climb on board and extensive records were kept. But Hastert's tough January talk gave way to spring and summer silence. The House ethics bill that passed in March only proposed to cut off privately financed travel for lawmakers for the rest of the year, after which the issue was supposed to be sorted out by the House Ethics Committee, which did virtually nothing in 2005, and is virtually moribund.

The Revolving Door

Among the practices denounced as sleaziest by public interest groups is the rapid spinning of the revolving door between the public and private sectors. If Members of Congress and key government officials are planning to leave public life to work for companies they regulate or oversee, they have a strong incentive to skew decisions in favor of those companies while in government. Members of Congress as well as most senior executive branch officials are currently [as of 2006] prohibited from making lobbying contacts or conducting lobbying activities for compensation for one year after leaving their positions. The public interest groups proposed extending the prohibition for two years.

According to Public Citizen, of the 198 Members who left Congress since 1998 and were eligible to lobby, 43 percent have since become lobbyists, including half of eligible ex-senators and 42 percent of ex-representatives.

Examples include ex-Speaker Bob Livingston, R-Louisiana, who built his business into one of the dozen largest non-law lobby firms in Washington.

Another is former Representative Billy Tauzin, R-Louisiana, who left his position as chair of the House Energy and Commerce Committee to take over a $2 million-a-year position as head of the pharmaceutical industry's lobby shop (PhRMA, the Pharmaceutical Research and Manufacturers of America). Shortly before leaving office, Tauzin helped shepherd through Congress the Medicare prescription drug bill, which was crafted with a host of industry-friendly provisions, including a prohibition on the government negotiating the prices of drugs it buys under the program.

"Congress has become a way station to wealth," says Joan Claybrook, president of Public Citizen. "Members use it for job training and networking so they can leave office and cash in on the connections they forged as elected officials. Lobbying has become the top career choice for departing Members."

'I don't believe lobbying reform's the problem,' Senator Tom Coburn, R-Oklahoma, explained. 'I believe Congress is. The problem is us.'

Republicans Stop Reform Efforts

Concerns about the revolving door were taken up by the Democrats, whose Honest Leadership and Open Government Act proposed to extend the existing lobbying ban for Members of Congress, as well as former senior executive personnel, from one to two years after they leave government. Their proposal also sought to eliminate floor privileges for any former senator or senator-elect who is a registered lobbyist and to require Members and their staff to report any ongoing employment negotiations. The Republican leadership blocked these proposals from going anywhere.

At the top of the groups' list of demands was creation of an independent Office of Public Integrity (OPI) to oversee and enforce ethics rules and lobbying laws, along with tougher penalties for violations. Currently [as of 2006], there is little to no independent monitoring or prosecution of fraudulent disclosure reports. The Congress' willingness to strengthen enforcement of the existing rules was considered by most observers to be the acid test of how serious it is about ethics and lobby reform.

This proposal too appeared in the Democrats' bill, but went nowhere. Craig Holman of Public Citizen's Congress Watch says the Senate Homeland Security Committee was most aggressive in attacking the Office of Public Integrity. Leading the attack was Senator George Voinovich, R-Ohio, who suggested that the Senate Ethics Committee was already doing its job. When Senators John McCain, R-Arizona, Russell Feingold, D-Wisconsin, and Barack Obama, D-Illinois, brought it up again for consideration from the floor, it was defeated by a 2-to-1 margin.

The Democrats did end up putting forward a strong reform package in the Honest Leadership and Open Government Act of 2006. In addition to the revolving door and Office of Public Integrity provisions, it would have strengthened lobbyist disclosure requirements, banned gifts from lobbyists and prohibited them from funding congressional travel, and cleaned up the contracting process by mandating competitive bidding and suspending unethical contractors. Forty senators—all but a handful of Senate Democrats—and 162 Members of the House of Representatives sponsored the bill.

In the Senate, the bill never made it out of the Homeland Security and Government Affairs Committee. "I don't believe lobbying reform's the problem," Senator Tom Coburn, R-Oklahoma, explained. "I believe Congress is. The problem is us. And transparency and reporting solves all that; not more rules, not more pads, not more things to mark down."

Some of the key provisions of the Democratic package were brought up as amendments on the Senate floor, where they were also defeated.

In the House, where Republicans routinely refuse to permit votes on Democratic proposals, the bill fared even worse, never coming up for a vote.

House Republicans consistently opposed provisions that could have a "chilling effect on lobbying," as House Rules Chair David Dreier, R-California, explained after jettisoning a requirement that lobbyists list contacts with lawmakers, thereby watering down a bill requiring expanded disclosure, the last major reform to survive the House Republican gauntlet.

Meaningless Reforms Are Passed

Instead, the Republican leadership in both houses pushed through bills they hoped would immunize them from electoral charges of doing nothing on corruption—but which reform advocates denounced as near-meaningless.

In the House, the leadership pressed Republican Members hard to secure passage of the Lobbying Accountability and Transparency Act of 2006, which won approval by a narrow 217-213 vote. The bill focuses on earmarks—appropriations for narrow and specific purposes, usually inserted—by a single Member of Congress outside of the normal committee process—an issue that critics say is at best peripheral to the lobbying scandals. The bill's modest reform would require Members to attach their names to specific earmarks.

The bill "is an illusion designed to try to sell the idea that you're doing reform while holding on to all the perks and benefits that lobbyists provide to Members," says Fred Wertheimer, president of Democracy 21. "It's not going to sell to the public."

Moreover, the so-called earmark "reform" is riddled with weaknesses and loopholes, according to Scott Lilley, a former staffer to the House Appropriations Committee. He points out that a great many things that are now considered earmarks are not included in the disclosure requirement, including "plus ups" for specific budget accounts where the intended recipient is known to the agency but not mentioned by name in the Committee or Conference Report. "This is exactly the kind of earmark that Duke Cunningham won on behalf of Automated Data Conversion Systems and the MZM Corporation in return for the bribes the executives of those two companies paid him," Lilley explains.

Much of what we uncovered in the investigation was, unfortunately, the ordinary was of doing business in this town.

On the Senate side, the results were similarly disheartening for reform advocates: by a 90-to-8 vote, a weak lobby reform bill passed that ignores the worst abuses, instead focusing on weak proposals, including enhanced disclosure.

Neither party had clean hands, however. Leaders from both parties in the House agreed to remove provisions from the lobbying bill that would have curbed 527 groups—which are able to make unlimited electoral expenditures, so long as they do not coordinate with candidates. Although initially anticipated to favor Republicans dramatically, Democrats proved more adept at using 527s in the 2004 elections.

Electoral Consequences

Without any major reforms in the cards, most observers see the scandals themselves as pieces in a larger political game: the fall [2006] elections.

Public opinion polls have suggested that the lobby scandals could damage the Republicans the most, but the Republicans are counting on their own ability to exploit bribery allegations surrounding Representative William Jefferson,

D-Louisiana, to muddy the waters should the topic of corruption in Congress become a major concern. But the fact that the Republicans are tied to Abramoff and control the Congress suggests that they have more to lose from an anti-incumbent backlash, and therefore more to gain by changing the topic.

Democratic activists especially hope that the Abramoff investigation will continue to expand, eventually reaching deep into the White House, while unraveling the shadowy network of K Street operatives thought to wield considerable power in the Republican Party.

The latter wish was given a little boost when Senator John McCain's Indian Affairs subcommittee released a report this spring, along with a series of emails implicating top K Street operatives Grover Norquist and Ralph Reed in the construction of an extensive network of non-profit groups that conspired to launder Indian tribal money for Abramoff.

"The Indian Affairs Committee has unearthed a story of excess and abuse," McCain explained. "Yet much of what we uncovered in the investigation was, unfortunately, the ordinary way of doing business in this town."

Norquist responded by suggesting that McCain was trying to get him back for siding with Bush during the 2000 primary campaign.

The Democrats at least must be relishing the fact that the Abramoff scandal has ignited this kind of partisan infighting on the other side, after years of exceptional Republican Party discipline and unity. Nevertheless, it's still unclear if the scandals can grow into something significant enough to cause a voter backlash that works to their benefit this fall. When Reed lost his primary bid for lieutenant governor of Georgia in July, party strategists on both sides suggested the scandals still have the potential to tip some key races, especially if new indictments are made between now and then.

Local Reforms

"We've seen the whole lobbying drive disintegrate before our eyes," says Craig Holman of Congress Watch. "It started out very slowly, then suddenly with the Jack Abramoff plea bargain it quickly picked up momentum and looked like we might be headed toward some fundamental reforms by March. But as the months rolled on you sensed the urgency fading away, and Congress getting more comfortable and secure in their positions. As time went on, the lobby reform proposals were whittled down to nothing. Which is what they are now essentially, just moderate increases in disclosure, but no restrictions on the real problem areas of lobbying activity."

"It amazes me, but I think most Members of Congress believe it's not an issue the American public will rebel over, that it's largely contrived by the press and that there isn't that much corruption on the Hill or in lobbying activities," Holman suggests.

For some advocates, the key is mobilizing popular support behind public financing of elections. They envision the march to reform as a long haul, which goes through the states before arriving in Washington.

The first steps, they say, have already been taken in states like Maine, Arizona and Connecticut, which have adopted clean elections laws mandating public financing. Another big step might come this fall in California, where a proposal for public financing of state elections will be put directly to the voters in a statewide initiative.

8

Efforts to Prevent Scandals Are Not Useless

Gary Ruskin

Gary Ruskin is the director of the Congressional Accountability Project and the executive director of Commercial Alert.

The problems with corruption, ethics abuses, and scandals in Congress run so deep that the majority of members may not be able to provide the necessary solutions. As of 2006, both Democrats and Republicans in Congress protect each other from everything but the most egregious ethics complaints. They would rather proceed with business as usual. However, key ideas, such as banning gifts from lobbyists and strengthening anti-bribery laws, are becoming part of the public discourse on politics. When the public is truly enraged by scandals, anything is possible— even ethics and corruption reform in Congress.

L et me introduce myself. Since 1993, I've run the Congressional Accountability Project, which opposes corruption in Congress. It hasn't been easy. I'll bet you understand. After thirteen years, I can't honestly claim any victories. Sure, some powerful members of Congress were embarrassed by front-page scandal stories. But it didn't do much good. Congress passed no major anti-corruption reforms. Here's why: Although both Republicans and Democrats are happy to hurl accusations at one another, neither has any real interest in reducing corruption in Congress.

Gary Ruskin, "No Housecleaning," *The Progressive*, vol. 70, May 2006, p. 22–25. Copyright © 2006 by The Progressive, Inc. Reproduced by permission of The Progressive, 409 East Main Street, Madison, WI 53703, www.progressive.org.

Even now, in the middle of the Jack Abramoff [2006] lobbying scandal, which may be the worst political scandal since Watergate, both parties are hoping that nobody notices when they pass sham reform and call it a triumph.

If you're keeping score, so far this year here's the only ethics reform the House has enacted: It has banned former members who are lobbyists from the House floor and the House gym. Yes, you read that right. And, yes, it's as pathetic as it sounds. Representative Martin Meehan, Democrat of Massachusetts, explains that it's "like putting a band-aid on a broken leg." The only effect, says lobbyist Tom Downey, will be boring basketball games. "If they ban former members, who's going to pass the ball?"

As for the Senate, on March 29 [2006] it passed an anemic bill that would force lobbyists to disclose more about their activities and would double the "cooling-off" period for members of Congress who become lobbyists. While the bill was titled the Legislative Transparency and Accountability Act, it should really be known as the Big Wet Kiss for Lobbyists Act. It's likely, though, that the Senate will have to revisit ethics reform later in the year, as the Abramoff scandal mounts, and elections approach.

When I hear Democratic Party leaders throwing around terms like 'culture of corruption,' I have to think: 'You oughta know.'

The GOP response to the Abramoff scandal started badly, and it's been downhill ever since. On January 17, Speaker Dennis Hastert and Rules Committee Chairman David Dreier, Republican of California, stepped to the podium to explain the House GOP's new ethics proposals. (Hastert is an imperfect spokesman on ethics, given his narrow escape in a bribery scandal regarding an alleged $100,000 offer to former Representative Nick Smith on the House floor in exchange for his vote on the Medicare drug bill.) Not surprisingly, their pro-posal was soft on corruption.

"Business as Usual"

In Washington, Republicans are the party of the corporations and their trade associations. Anti-corruption reforms threaten corporations because they reduce the influence of money in politics. If money can't buy legislative action, then corpora-tions won't get what they want. Lobbying reforms also cut into those lovely perks that members of Congress crave.

So, Hastert and Dreier played it safe, calling for a ban on privately paid congressional travel, stricter gift rules, doubling the current one-year period during which former members and staff can't lobby their former colleagues, and requiring former members to forfeit their pensions if convicted of a felony related to their congressional duties.

But even that was too tough for the Free Lunch Caucus. Before becoming House majority leader, John Boehner called the proposed ban on privately sponsored travel "childish." Senator Trent Lott (who chairs the Senate Committee on Rules and Administration, which has jurisdiction over many of the reforms) called some of the reforms "outrageous." He added: "I mean, now we're going to say you can't have a meal for more than $20. Where you going to—to McDonald's?"

Now that Boehner is majority leader, real reform is look-ing less likely. On national TV, in a spasm of denial, Boehner said that "taking actions to ban this and ban that, when there's no appearance of a problem, there's no foundation of a prob-lem, I think, in fact, does not serve the institution well." Trans-lation: We love business as usual.

Amazingly, when the Democrats announced their ethics plan, it was almost as tame as the Republicans'. It would double the one-year lobbying cooling-off period, strengthen lobbying disclosure and the enforcement of it, prohibit travel paid by lobbyists, and bar some gifts from lobbyists (but still allow those given in the context of political fundraising). Nothing in that package will win them a profile in courage.

In recent weeks [Spring 2006], the Democrats have adopted a new mantra: denouncing the Republican "culture of corruption." Majority Leader Boehner replies: "When I hear Democratic Party leaders throwing around terms like 'culture of corruption,' I have to think: 'You oughta know.'" And Boehner is right. Democrats didn't want to fix such corruption when they were in charge.

Democrats and Republicans Work Together to Prevent Reforms

I vividly remember seeking campaign finance, lobbying, and gift reform in 1993–1994, when Democrats controlled Congress and the White House. At that time, Speaker Tom Foley shut down all reform—and made Gingrich's revolution possible. Foley was comfortable with the corruption; it kept his party in power, and in perks.

Democrats haven't changed much since then. They have the power to file ethics complaints to trigger investigations of Republican corruption. But they don't. Here's a dirty secret: House Minority Leader Nancy Pelosi basically prohibits her Democrats from filing ethics complaints against Republicans— even powerful ones. In other words, Pelosi protects Republicans from investigations of corruption, influence-peddling, and abuse of power.

The "reforms" created a climate in Congress where corruption is increasingly possible—exactly what both parties wanted.

Why does Pelosi act as the Republicans' angel of mercy? If Democrats filed ethics complaints, Republicans would, too. The likely result of such an "ethics war": Corruption would be exposed, members from both parties would be embarrassed, and a few might lose their seats in Congress. There might even be an indictment or two. Maybe someone would go to jail. Sounds great. But it's intolerable to both parties. So, for nearly ten years, both parties have conspired to make an ethics "truce" and have rarely filed complaints against each other.

Ethics complaints are important, because they trigger at least a preliminary investigation into possible corruption by members of Congress. I've probably filed more of them than anyone. And I was the last non-House member to file one against a House member. In September 1996, I filed complaints against two very powerful Republicans: Tom DeLay (then House majority whip) and Bud Shuster of Pennsylvania (then chairman of the House Transportation Committee).

Neither Republicans nor Democrats could tolerate it any longer. Because of the complaints, too many powerful members of Congress looked bad in their local newspapers.

You can probably guess what happened. The House, by agreement of both Republicans and Democrats, for nine months instituted an "ethics moratorium" during which ethics complaints and investigations were prohibited. Then, in September 1997, they passed "reforms" (I called them the Corrupt Politicians' Protection Act) that made it impossible for citizens to file ethics complaints in the House. The "reforms" created a climate in Congress where corruption is increasingly possible—exactly what both parties wanted. And it nearly put the Congressional Accountability Project out of business because we couldn't file complaints in the House anymore. Mission accomplished: a House of Representatives safe for the likes of Randy "Duke" Cunningham [Republican representative, now convicted of taking bribes] and Jack Abramoff.

Sometimes we reformers joke that Congress isn't really for sale, because the current owners are quite pleased with it.

That pretty well sums up the problem.

So, what's the solution?

How to Solve Congressional Ethics Scandals

In early January, we at Commercial Alert proposed the Honest Government Agenda, a set of fifteen reforms. The key ones are:

Ban Gifts. Members of Congress and their staff should be prohibited from accepting for private benefit any gifts from lobbyists or the general public.

Strengthen the Anti-Bribery and Gratuity Statutes. In 1999, the Supreme Court knocked a major loophole in the federal illegal gratuities law, making it harder to prosecute politicians who take gifts from favor-seekers like Jack Abramoff. Congress should strengthen federal anti-bribery and gratuity laws to prohibit special interests from using gifts to curry favor with public officials.

When voters get really angry, members of Congress get really scared. And when they're scared, anything is possible.

Prohibit the Purchase of Influence. The House and Senate should pass ethics rules to prohibit members of Congress from providing influence or official action in exchange for campaign contributions of other consideration.

Overhaul the Congressional Ethics Process. New rules are meaningless without enforcement. The House and Senate ethics committees have been hesitant to investigate powerful members of Congress and to punish wrongdoing. Congress should invigorate the House and Senate ethics committees by ensuring that outside counsel will investigate ethics complaints against members of Congress, restoring citizens' ability to file ethics complaints in the House, and making the ethics process more transparent.

Pass Public Campaign Financing. You need a lot of money to displace a corrupt member of Congress, and many challengers can't raise it. Broadcasters should be required to provide free or reduced cost TV and radio ads for candidates for federal office. (This is the most effective reform; therefore, it's also the most unlikely.)

Right now, the smart money is betting that none of these reforms will pass. Or even come close.

The good news is there are earnest reformers in Congress, like Senator John McCain, Senator Russ Feingold, Representative Chris Shays, and Representative Martin Meehan. They deserve our respect. They're doing their best.

I do believe that in the end, these public servants are going to deliver us a big victory. Why? Three reasons.

First, because the Abramoff scandal is just too big to be swept under the rug.

Second, because I don't think McCain is going to accept defeat. He is more talented, tenacious, resourceful, and determined than most people know.

Third, and most important, I don't think that the American people will tolerate the drumbeat of Abramoff news stories without real anti-corruption reforms.

When voters get really angry, members of Congress get really scared. And when they're sacred, anything is possible.

9

Ethics Laws Can Instill Public Trust

Nicole Casal Moore

Nicole Casal Moore is a writer and researcher for the National Conference of State Legislatures.

In the wake of ethics scandals, state legislatures have enacted a variety of reforms to restore public trust in local government. Major scandals in Washington, DC, tend to trickle down to the state and local level, affecting public confidence in all levels of government. The most important reform government can take is to increase the level of transparency so the public can see all of the inner workings and understand what is going on.

They have names like Shrimpscam, Azcam, Bop Trot, Operation Lost Trust, Tennessee Waltz. They are investigations into political corruption and ethics violations that snare legislators and damage legislatures. In 2005, scandals in at least six states involved lawmakers. The fallout can be devastating to public perception and confidence and sullies the reputation of the institution and those who serve in it. That's when ethics reform takes center stage.

In the year since four Tennessee lawmakers and others were arrested in a bribery sting and charged with extortion, their former colleagues in the [Tennessee] General Assembly have been busy enacting new ethics laws.

Nicole Casal Moore, "Flexing the Ethics Muscle: Restoring Public Confidence in Government After a Scandal Is a Legislature's Prime Goal," *State Legislatures*, vol. 32, July–August 2006, p. 24. www.ncsl.org/programs/pubs/slmag/2006/06SLJulAug06 _EthicsMuscle.pdf. Copyright © 2006 National Conference of State Legislatures. Reproduced by permission.

Leaders appointed a bipartisan, joint ethics committee and called [state] legislators into a special session where they created a new ethics commission with broad jurisdiction over lawmakers. They banned lobbyists from giving lawmakers campaign contributions or gifts. And they required lobbyists to report more details about their finances. These are among the more visible of the many ethics and lobbying provisions Tennessee legislators passed late last year and in early 2006.

But none of them would have prevented the scandal of 2005. Those crimes were already against the law, points out Tennessee Senator Jim Kyle, a member of the joint ethics committee that wrote the bills. So why did the legislature pass them? "We felt that if we didn't exceed the public's expectations, we could lose the moral authority to govern," Kyle says.

A January 2006 Harris poll found that only 4 percent of U.S. adults believe the Abramoff scandal is an isolated case, compared to 86 percent who think he is just one of many who happened to get caught.

Though initiated in response to scandals, Tennessee's new laws aim for a higher purpose—to help restore public confidence in government.

And Tennessee is not alone. Connecticut, Florida, North Carolina and other states reacted to scandals in the last few years that legislators felt violated the public trust.

Reform, or Lose Public Trust

State legislators across the nation have introduced close to 200 ethics and lobbying bills so far this year [summer 2006]. At press time, five states—Colorado, Iowa, Maine, Tennessee and Virginia—had enacted new laws, with Tennessee's overhaul the most significant. It's too early to tell whether this will be a banner year for ethics reform. Some factors suggest that it might be. It's an election year. And the federal scandal involving former lobbyist Jack Abramoff and several members of Congress has cast a shadow over government.

A January 2006 Harris poll found that only 4 percent of U.S. adults believe the Abramoff scandal is an isolated case, compared to 86 percent who think he is just one of many who happened to get caught.

There's likely a connection between the Abramoff scandal and the long list of ethics bills being considered in state legislatures—75 of which deal with lobbying. It was behind Minnesota Senator Linda Higgins' ethics bill, which, among other things, would require more financial disclosure by lobbyists and would establish a two-year period before former legislators may lobby. The bill's purpose is to ensure the public knows how lobbyists are influencing the legislative process.

"I looked at the Abramoff scandal and thought that, even though it's in Washington, people might start to look at us and think maybe our branch of government is like that," Higgins says. "Maybe we also were getting golfing trips to Scotland paid by lobbyists. Yet in Minnesota, we can't even take a cup of coffee from lobbyists."

National Scandals Affect Local Government

Robert Stern, president of the bipartisan Center for Governmental Studies in Los Angeles, understands this umbrella effect. "The public puts everyone in the same field and doesn't distinguish among the various levels of government," he says. "If the president and the Congress are seen in a bad light, so is every other public official."

Stern says legislatures rarely pass campaign finance or ethics laws unless there's been a scandal at some level of government. But, he says, we can't have a law for every situation. "There should be a standard that says you shouldn't embarrass the body."

Connecticut lawmakers were embarrassed not only by the misconduct of their governor, John Rowland, but by the inability of the State Ethics Commission to respond to it. Many of the commissioners recused themselves from the bribery investigations citing conflicts of interest with the former governor, who was ultimately sentenced to a year in prison.

The legislature passed laws in 2005 subjecting contractors to state ethics laws, including gift limitations and reporting requirements. It also abolished the nine-member ethics commission and fired its director. Now the state has an Office of State Ethics, with a Citizens' Ethics Advisory Board.

Not all ethics reforms are the direct result of headline-grabbing scandals. There hasn't been an FBI sting in North Carolina, but there has been a flurry of allegations over the past several years that lawmakers wanted to address. They formed an ethics study commission which, according to House Majority Leader Joe Hackney, who co-chaired it, succeeded in elevating the discussion of ethics, as it looked at the areas of lobbying and campaign finance. "We recommended 10 bills—a good package," he says.

Representative Hackney says that most members of the legislature are vigilant. "They do not violate our ethics laws," he says. "But we need these laws to tell the public that we mean business."

Florida tackled public perception when it enacted in late 2006 what Senate President Tom Lee calls "some of the boldest lobbying reforms in the nation."

Lee says he has always been uncomfortable with the "wining and dining" that takes place at receptions and events sponsored by lobbyists. "I saw how much money was being spent to influence how our laws were being made," he says. And even though the events were perfectly legal, they "just never seemed right."

He says he set out to change the cozy relationship between lawmakers and lobbyists because he believes it precluded the people from having a voice. Lee says the desired effect of the Florida laws was to give grassroots and constituent groups a more level playing field "without having to bear big checks or perks to gain admission to the process."

Ethics are like a muscle. They have to be used or they get a little soft.

Lee says it's not always easy for legislators to support ethics legislation. The "gift-giving culture" can be very offended, he says. The new Florida law, which bans lobbyists from giving gifts or hospitality to legislators, is being challenged in federal court by the Florida Association of Professional Lobbyists who protests its requirement to report compensation.

Do Ethics Laws Work?

What good are ethics laws? Do they increase the public's trust in government? Ironically, Americans' confidence in government has receded while legislatures have passed more and more ethics laws. According to the American National Election Studies' biennial poll, which tracks citizen confidence in government, public trust declined from more than 60 percent in the early 1960s to less than 30 percent by the year 2000. These aren't numbers to be proud of, but where would they be if legislatures had not focused on ethics?

Tennessee Representative Kyle says there has been a noticeable change in Tennessee since the legislature enacted ethics reform. He admits that there is still a fair amount of cynicism, but "as a whole, and I can only tell from my constituent communications, it's getting better. The tone has changed," he says.

Kyle says the FBI sting was a wake-up call. "It caused us to take a look at ourselves and see where we were in comparison to other states with citizen legislatures. When you go through this experience, it makes you reflect."

Transparency Can Build Trust

Many citizens may not trust their government today, but at least they can verify certain pieces of information, thanks to laws that require open meetings and legislators to disclose their economic interests.

Transparency is the word of the day, says Courtney Pearre, president of the Tennessee Lobbyist Association. New disclosure laws in Tennessee provide more windows through which its residents can observe the political process.

"I think this type of legislation is good for improving the perception, or really the reality of how the process works," Pearre says. "There is more reporting. There are more limitations on what lobbyists can do and what legislators can do, so I think everyone feels better about it."

In many states, disclosure by legislators and lobbyists is the answer to conflicts of interest. Forty-seven states require legislators to file regular financial disclosure forms showing the sources, and in some cases, the amounts, of outside income, as well as other details about property holdings and investments. This session [in 2006], 26 states considered or are considering ethics legislation dealing with some aspect of disclosure.

In addition to reporting financial conflicts, rules in 66 of the nation's 99 legislative chambers require lawmakers to reveal any conflicts of interest they have with matters at hand either before abstaining from voting, before voting, or shortly after voting.

But disclosure doesn't erase the conflict, says Utah Representative David Clark. "Lawmakers should decide on their core values and use them to create a template to place over ethical decisions." Legislators often have conflicts of interest, Clark says. "It's how you handle them that counts.

"Ethics are like a muscle. They have to be used or they get a little soft," he says.

And when legislators flex their ethical muscle, they're strengthening public confidence, which Senator Lee says is vital to our system of government.

"The most important thing we can do as public officials is to enhance the public trust," Lee says. "It's at the core of our democracy. Democracy can't function if people don't trust their elected officials."

10

Instituting Public Campaign Financing Can Reduce Political Scandals

Mark Schmitt

Mark Schmitt is a senior fellow at the New America Foundation.

In the wake of political scandals, politicians suggest limits on various elements of the political process. However, the way to reduce political scandals is not to try more limits—which have not worked in the past—but to strengthen the voices of political challengers. Elections are the ultimate time for voters to express their opinions regarding their elected officials, but too often voters do not hear the other sides of the stories, as political challengers are drowned out by privately financed incumbents. When political challengers can be heard, incumbents will have an incentive to avoid scandals.

Our long national nightmare has just begun. There is now little doubt that the next three years will bring one revelation after another about the magnitude of congressional corruption. Democrats will relish this prospect, and "reform" will be an inevitable theme of the next two election cycles. But some political scandals lead to change, while others dominate the headlines for a year and leave no trace. Why? Some of it has to do with managing the media, but it also involves offering credible solutions. Scandals without solutions simply stoke public cynicism. And it is in just such cynical soil that the seed of corrupt big-government "conservatism" was planted.

Mark Schmitt, "The Limits of Limits," *The American Prospect*, vol. 17, no. 3, March 1, 2006, p. 8. www.newamerica.net/publications/articles/2006/the_limits_of_limits. Copyright 2006 *The American Prospect*, Inc. All rights reserved. Reproduced with permission from *The American Prospect*, 11 Beacon Street, Suite 1120, Boston, MA 02108.

The challenge, then, is to define the solution. The first bid, from some Republicans and from overly literal Democrats, will be "lobbying reform." Keeping lobbyists at arm's length should be a matter of personal responsibility on the part of elected officials, reinforced by clear rules. But the idea that the large-scale wrongdoing we've witnessed recently [as of March 2006] could have been prevented by banning lobbyists from paying for lunch or trips is laughable.

The problem isn't who pays for lunch. It's who pays for politics. Elected officials with enough integrity can skip the meals and trips. But none of them can avoid the lobbyists who control, directly or indirectly, much of the money that pays for elections.

The more far-reaching proposals for reform acknowledge this fact and call for limits on contributions from lobbyists, limits on fund-raisers hosted by lobbyists, and limits on independent political committees. Some of these provisions are wise, some unconstitutional, others easily evaded. And what they have in common is: They are all based on limits.

Limits address only one side of the relationship between political money and corruption. There's another dimension where there isn't enough money in politics.

Why Don't Spending Limits Work?

But limits have reached their own limits. Almost four years after passage of the McCain-Feingold law, its modest limits on soft money and certain issue ads are still contested, or, in the case of political use of the Internet, seem to have spun down a regulatory rabbit hole. Unless the Supreme Court this year [2006] decides to uphold a Vermont law imposing mandatory limits on spending—which would be a surprise—limits on contributions will coexist with unlimited spending, which inevitably creates further pressure and incentive to find ways

69

around the existing limits. As long as we have a Constitution and capitalism, there will be ways.

Limits address only one side of the relationship between political money and corruption. There's another dimension where there isn't enough money in politics. And that's where the connection to the current scandals is strongest and where real solutions are possible.

Let's walk this scandal back: As George W. Bush says, there is only one "accountability moment" for an elected official—Election Day. And for almost all the members of Congress involved in these scandals, that moment passed no differently from any other November Tuesday. Ohio Representative Bob Ney, "Representative #1" in the Jack Abramoff indictment, won his last reelection outspending his opponent $1.4, million to $18,000. John Doolittle of California, another who intervened on behalf of Abramoff clients, spent less than Ney; but his last two opponents *combined* had only $10,000.

It's on the second number rather than the first that reform must focus. Imagine if Ney's opponent had $500,000—enough to hire a research staff and buy some radio ads raising questions about, for example, the odd statements that Ney introduced into the Congressional Record in support of Abramoff's casino-boat franchise. Is it possible that might have wiped a little of the smirk off Ney's face?

Tough Elections Will Prevent Scandals

The next generation of campaign finance laws has to involve not more limits, but expansive reform that strengthens the voice of challengers and enhances the power of small donors. None of this is fantasy; public-financing systems in Arizona, Maine, New York City, Minnesota, and now Connecticut, though varying greatly in their details, all make it easier to run and be heard.

These systems don't overreach; they don't try to ban all private money; close every loophole, make every election perfectly competitive, or force a constitutional showdown. They aren't rigged to change the partisan balance, either. But all these systems do allow candidates with a broad base of public support from small donors, but without great personal wealth or big-dollar backers, to be heard.

It's easy to waver between total cynicism and overambitious optimism on this issue. Yes, there will always be corrupting influences. But these next-generation reforms might, among other benefits, remind elected officials that they can no longer operate in a zone of silence, confident that their actions will go unchallenged. And that just might force those with power to think twice before abusing it as they did in the current [2006] mega-scandal.

11

Journalists Should Lessen Their Coverage of Political Scandals

Matthew Felling

Matthew Felling is the media director at the Center for Media and Public Affairs, a policy institute in Washington, DC.

The media have learned that scandalous stories are profitable, but stories involving the misdeeds of elected officials can be both profitable and in the public's interest. The media do not need to adopt confusing standards, but rather judge politicians based on the rule of law and their own professed beliefs. Furthermore, the media should focus on individuals with particular value to the general public and people who interact with the media on a professional basis. The media should stop covering personal scandals merely because a celebrity is involved or because a story seems like good gossip.

Few newspaper stories linger in the mind days, weeks, or even years after being printed. But of the ones that do, most originate in international conflict, political races, or scandal.

Scandal journalism is big business unto itself. It is profitable titillation focusing on greed, lust, and all evils that men do, guaranteeing a large and voracious audience. But this muckraking is not limited to the publications that loom over grocery-store checkout counters. Yellow journalism and rumormongering are becoming a part of the mainstream media.

There are at least two major scandal categories: one involving famous people and one in which the people involved become famous because of the scandal. An example of this distinction is the O.J. Simpson murder trial versus the JonBenet Ramsey killing.

Any story involving celebrity public figures immediately acquires the stamp of newsworthiness. People, including journalists, generally assume (perhaps erroneously) that because famous people are important, the story itself is important. This effectively hands major media outlets a ready-made reason for providing the public with every minute detail of the lives of the parties involved. (Remember Rep. Gary Condit's penchant for Ben & Jerry's ice cream?)

[W]hen a big "car wreck" of a scandal story occurs, the news flow can often slow to a crawl.

Of course, what is relevant to one journalist (or reader) can be considered offensive by another. Are there any guidelines in the newsroom? Not according to Howard Kurtz of the *Washington Post*, who wrote in his book *Media Circus* that "the plain truth is that there are no rules anymore, no corner of human behavior into which prying reporters won't poke." Salacious tidbits aren't solely in the domain of the *National Enquirer*, he continues. "All of the media, from the prestige press to the sensationalist rags, have been infected by a tabloid culture that celebrates sleaze."

Scandalous Stories Are Profitable

The tendency of newsmen to dig into public figures' private lives is constantly lamented by readers, viewers, ethicists—and even media professionals like Kurtz. But protest as we may against the practice, it caters to our voyeuristic instinct and ensures high ratings and circulation numbers. When you combine a competitive advertising market with media coverage decisions increasingly being made in corporate boardrooms rather than newsrooms, such stories prove too tempting to withstand.

This can be called rubberneck journalism. Like traffic, news—local, national, political, weather, business, and so forth—flows along a certain path in a constant pattern. Just as in traffic we ultimately get to our destination, in consuming the regular flow of news we find out all we need to know. But when a big "car wreck" of a scandal story occurs, the news flow can often slow to a crawl. Everyone peers over with morbid curiosity, visually poring over the broken glass and carnage. Though we have places to go and people to see, the pull of the wreck is too strong for many to resist—and too profitable for the media to push us away from.

The core problem with rubberneck journalism is that it distracts journalists from waving us along like police officers, getting us to the next story. All too often, they call our attention to different aspects of the wreck, hardly encouraging us to move on.

This problem will not diminish unless we start asking some important questions: How can scandal journalism be constrained? What kinds of guidelines could the media use for covering the private lives of public figures? Journalists are understandably wary of restrictions that impede press freedom, but they may be open to some agreed-upon standards to maintain the quality of journalistic content. After all, it's not just the public figures who take a hit when a scandal breaks. Though the public avidly gobbles up all the gossipy tidbits, it still holds the media in low regard when they indulge in such frenzies.

Deborah Potter of the Poynter Institute notes that "while the public claims not to care about [a scandal story], and complains that it's been overdone, newspaper sales and ratings [are] bumped up substantially. 'I can't stand it,' readers and viewers seem to be saying, 'tell me more!'" So it's a paradox:

The public devours such lurid tales as it laments the prevalence of such fare, but it's in the best interest of the journalistic profession and consumers to make some changes.

Journalists Should Go Back to the Basics

The following suggestions on covering public figures' private lives are laid out in categories drawn from Journalism 101: who, how, and what.

Before examining how the media cover public figures, we must answer the very basic question: Who is a public figure? For the sake of this article, we'll focus solely on individuals within the political realm—candidates or elected officials, their staffers, and relatives.

One good way of deciding whether a person is a public figure worthy of coverage is to note whether he has actively attempted to use the media to his personal or professional advantage. The most crucial application of this standard is with politicians' family members.

[T]he most dismaying aspect of scandal coverage is the lack of clear rules and the frequent appearance of double standards.

Let's compare two famous relatives of Bill Clinton. Roger Clinton, the president's brother, tried to parlay Bill's success into singing contracts and paid appearances. This made him a public figure both through association and through a calculated effort on his part. Then, when the media exposed his criminal history and drug problems, the Clinton family cried foul.

Chelsea Clinton was often seen at public events with her famous parents. While making her a public figure through association, it was a fact beyond her control. When the media tried to find out about teenage crushes, high-school grades, and behavior, the Clinton family again cried foul.

Using the above standard, Roger Clinton solicited media attention only when it was convenient, asking for its spotlight to further his fledgling entertainment career. But he wanted only the media's soft, flattering light, not the glaring lamp that exposed his run-ins with the law. One can't have it both ways. Roger was fair game.

Chelsea, on the other hand, was a reluctant public figure—like many presidents' children. Barely uttering a peep publicly, she was not a self-promoter. She seemed a Garboesque adolescent, just wanting to be left alone. Using the above standard, the media went too far in trying to dig into details of her private life.

This basic premise can easily extend to other families. Jenna and Laura Bush seem to be following in Chelsea's footsteps by keeping a very low profile. The press, following the above rule, should have held back on their saturation coverage of the sisters' underage margarita purchase last year. On the other hand, Ronald Reagan Jr. parlayed his famous parentage connection into an embarrassing array of film and television roles.

The Gray Areas of Public Life

Are there gray areas in this approach? Sure, as in cases of low-profile public figures who engage in extreme criminal and unethical behavior. But it is a valuable and fair first step in gauging which celebrities are off-limits to coverage.

In a utopian world, we would have universal rules that are adhered to by all media. To athletes and sports fans, there are few things more irritating than inconsistent officiating. Why, they say, is one player's shove permissible but his opponent's identical nudge a penalty? Similarly, the most dismaying aspect of scandal coverage is the lack of clear rules and frequent appearance of double standards.

Thus, there needs to be a single, nationwide set of standards accepted by all (or at least most) journalists and applied universally. From the *Sacramento Bee* to the *Wall Street Journal*, newspeople need to shake hands and agree on some basic rules. Otherwise we'll be left in the current muck of talking heads and apologists issuing polemics at one apparent breach of journalistic ethics, only to utilize the opposite argument when it suits their needs.

A major suggestion is as follows: Let the media allow the politicians to dictate the standards with which they will be judged. Occasionally, a politician defiantly dares journalists to dig all the dirt they want. A few examples come easily to mind, such as Democratic candidate Gary Hart's 1988 challenge to campaign reporters. Sometimes this defiance is stated even more strongly, as when South Carolina Gov. David Beasley replied to rumors that he was involved in an inappropriate relationship with a senior staffer. "If I fail in that standard, I want you to knock my teeth out. I want you to rip me up and down this state. I want you to embarrass me, humiliate me, and destroy me, because I will have done wrong."

Identity Check

Whether or not the media are invited or challenged to investigate public figures' private lives, they will continue doing so. How about a very basic ground rule?

One suggestion is holding politicians to an ethical standard based on their "signature" issues and public persona. It could be called the "identity check," because, just as politicians take up various economic, trade, or crime issues and are held accountable for their expertise and accomplishments on them, they usually take identifiable positions in areas like family values, drugs, and clean government. As Larry Sabato, Mark Stencel, and Robert Lichter, authors of *Peepshow Media and Politics in an Age of Scandal*, say: "In this age of moral inexactitude and situational ethics it is easy to understand why candidates choose to emphasize 'family values.' . . . It is less easy to understand why candidates with messy personal lives choose to [do so]."

Using the same rationale applied to Roger Clinton, politicians should be particularly scrutinized on the issues that they use to call attention to themselves.

But journalists can't monitor every public utterance. After all, politicians speak every day on nearly every topic under the sun. How can the media single out signature issues amid a sea of Rotary Club remarks and press releases? Journalists could focus on the issues that a politician stresses during election years. This would provide newsmen with an ironclad reason for making a private issue public. Any issue that a reporter can extract from a campaign speech—the quintessential laundry list of things that a candidate wants to be known for—is germain.

The same criticism leveled against politicians for breaking campaign promises should be warranted when they don't live up to their word on a personal level. The most elementary starting point is an "identity check" on the personal level. Like their pet issues, politicians often define personal virtues they believe in or behavior they condemn. These are the issues that the media should be allowed to examine with gusto.

Disarming Nosy Reporters

In addition to solidifying what is currently shaky ethical ground for journalists, this standard would also provide a means for politicians to disarm nosy reporters. If an elected official is asked about a personal matter, he would have the right to look the reporter in the eye and say, "I have never asked my constituents to judge me on such touchy personal matters and do not want to enter into that discussion now." Obviously, if the matter at hand was similar to one he had vilified others for, such a response would not be condoned.

Some would say that the "campaign year" loophole is too wide. For example, what of a senator who rails against infidelity for five years but quietly tucks the issue away on the campaign trail? (As if such a glaring omission could evade a ravenous media corps!) Such concerns are moot in today's media environment, where 24-hour channels are yawning vacuums that need to be filled and journalists are hungry to break stories. What reporter is going to overlook such a gaping hole in a candidate's rhetoric during an election year?

Are there difficult issues? Surely. What to make of statutes of limitations? Aren't people allowed to change their stands over time? What about behavior so verboten that it doesn't even merit mentioning in speeches? All these things can be discussed in the future as we hone the ethics of media investigations to a sharp edge.

Once politicos try to use the media as a blade to cut their path in the world of government, they must realize better than they now do that they, too, can be cut by it. An industry-wide pact to develop this type of journalism would lead to a decline in nauseating feeding frenzies, and it might even result in wiser, more careful candidates for the public to support.

13

Hypocrisy Causes Political Scandals

David Paul Kuhn and John F. Harris

As of 2007 David Paul Kuhn is the senior political news writer for CBSNews.com; John F. Harris was a White House correspondent for the Washington Post.

Hypocritical behavior by politicians leads to public outrage, which creates political scandals. In particular, politicians who uphold a particularly high moral standard are vulnerable to scandals if they engage in behavior they otherwise would not condone. Politicians who have said one thing while doing another have suffered in the media and lost the support of the public as well as that of social or other political leaders.

Lust, predation, hypocrisy. These behaviors were observed in humans, including Washington politicians, even before Republicans roared to power on Capitol Hill in the 1990s.

But the agony of Sen. David Vitter (R-La)—a self-proclaimed social conservative exposed [July 9, 2007] as a customer of an escort service—is one more float in a long and flamboyant parade of sexual follies and scandals served up by his generation of congressional Republicans. Previous attractions include former House members Newt Gingrich, Henry Hyde, Bob Barr, Bob Livingston and Mark Foley.

Embarrassment for the GOP was entertainment for many others, as people in Washington and around the nation

David Paul Kuhn and John F. Harris, "GOP Fears for Credibility after Scandals," Politico.com, July 11, 2007. www.politico.com/news/stories/0707/4873.html. Reproduced by permission.

chortled over the latest stubbed toe for a crowd that took power, and held it, in large measure by decrying the decay of traditional values and by issuing censorious attacks on the personal failings of political rivals.

Beyond the chortling, however, the Vitter scandal is a small piece of a much more significant development: The demoralized state of the social conservative movement on the brink of the 2008 election.

The Public Rejects Hypocrisy

"It's the hypocrisy that people can't stand," said Michael Cromartie, a social conservative himself who chaired the U.S. Commission on International Religious Freedom under President Bush. "It's not the fact that people are frail and given to sinful behavior. It's when they try to pretend to be morally upright and end up being self-righteous because they preach one thing and live another."

The gulf between the professed values of conservative political leaders and the way some actually conduct their lives has sapped energy from a movement that was a powerful engine for the Republican Party over the past three decades.

This gap is shadowing the presidential race. The GOP presidential contest so far has not featured any full-blown tabloid sex scandals.

Yet many social conservative leaders have made clear their ambivalent feelings about the top tier of declared and potential candidates—in part because of doubts that these politicians are genuinely sympathetic to the aims of their movement.

The modern social conservative movement grew in large measure as a reaction against the dominant cultural developments of the 1960s and 1970s.

Traditional values advocates opposed casual sex, divorce, tolerance of alternative lifestyles and the supposed liberal mind-set that dictated (in the famous phrase), "If it feels good, do it."

Do as I Say, Not as I Do

Many of this year's crop of candidates, however, have been enthusiastic beneficiaries of the sexual revolution and the more lenient cultural mores it ushered in.

Sen. John McCain (R-Ariz.), former Sen. Fred Thompson and former New York Mayor Rudy Giuliani have all been divorced—twice in the case of Giuliani. All have gone through phases in their lives in which they were known for fast-lane social lives.

All politicians' private lives should comport with their public policy.

Among the candidates waiting in the wings of the presidential race is former Speaker Gingrich, a man who has also been divorced twice and recently acknowledged that he was carrying on an affair at the same time he was leading the charge against Bill Clinton in the Monica Lewinsky scandal.

Like Gingrich, Vitter was a veteran of the GOP conference in the House before being elected to the Senate. This group also included Hyde (whose own "youthful indiscretion" came to light while he was a leader of impeachment proceedings against Clinton).

The political implications of sex scandals were made clear last fall. Many Republican strategists believe social conservative turnout was dampened by the problems of Florida's Foley, who was shown to have made predatory advances toward male interns.

Vitter apologized Monday night [July 2, 2007] after the phone records of the so-called "D.C. Madam" listed his telephone number. Vitter is the first member of Congress, and the second political insider, to be linked to a sex scandal that has dominated Washington scuttlebutt for months.

A Higher Standard

Social conservative leaders yesterday debated the implications of his behavior—and how stern to be in their own judgments about it.

"All politicians' private lives should comport with their public policy," said Pat Mahoney, director of the Christian Defense Coalition and a veteran social conservative activist. "Sen. Vitter is known for having very strong conservative moral values; that's what he's known for. Yes, [social conservatives] should be held to a higher standard.

"Is it hypocritical for any candidate like former Speaker Gingrich or Congressman Mark Foley, who actually worked on missing and sexually abused children?" Mahoney continued. "Yes, it is absolutely hypocritical and needs to be challenged."

But some voices said personal characteristics must be viewed in fair context—not as a one-strike-and-you're-out proposition.

"It is totally legitimate and even preferable for all voters to want to find men and women of good moral character who are running for office," said Gary Bauer, a former domestic policy adviser to Ronald Reagan and longtime social conservative leader.

"If a voter is looking for Jesus on the Republican ticket, they're not going to find him," Bauer continued. "There was only one perfect man, and all others have fallen short. They should look at how a candidate dealt with his moral failures."

Political Peril

But Bauer said he recognized the political peril of hypocritical behavior. "One of the dilemmas we have here is that the left has concluded that if they can find the moral mistake that conservative candidates have made they can peel off enough of the Christian vote to neutralize it," he said.

Meanwhile, the question of which presidential candidates social conservatives will rally around—if anyone—continues to percolate.

Giuliani has polled reasonably well among social conservatives, despite supporting abortion rights and gay rights—results that themselves indicate no traditional candidate is lighting the race on fire.

There is scant evidence that McCain is catching on among cultural conservatives, despite sharing their views against legal abortion.

Former Massachusetts Gov. Mitt Romney, whose views on abortion have shifted over time, now backs cultural conservatives on this and other social issues. In addition, by all evidence to date, he and his wife of 38 years have led highly traditional personal lives, raising five children.

But some GOP strategists have said he faces doubts among Christian conservatives because of unease about his Mormon faith.

"Giuliani and McCain clearly do not come from the social conservative movement," Cromartie said. "Thompson and Romney, at least in language and all the people I know they are surrounding themselves with, are trying to be." But Cromartie warns that "we'll see" whether any GOP candidate succeeds.

A Debate Over Values

One lower-tier GOP candidate said the discussion about how sincere politicians are in their professions to be social conservatives is fair—and it's a debate he welcomes.

"Many of us became a part of the Republican Party so that we could find a home for traditional beliefs regarding marriage and family and the sanctity of human life," said former Arkansas Gov. Mike Huckabee, who is also a Baptist minister.

"If those things really don't exist in the party, then we have to ask, 'Why are we here?' Yeah, I'm a fiscal conservative as well, but that's not the only thing that motivates many of us to be involved in politics."

14

Executive Privilege Is Abused in Recent Political Scandals

Bruce Fein

Bruce Fein is a constitutional lawyer and chairman of the American Freedom Agenda, a think tank.

Executive privilege has been used repeatedly by President George W. Bush to deny information needed for congressional investigations. In a political scandal involving the firing of U.S. attorneys, it appears that the use of executive privilege is intended to shield the White House from responsibility. Although executive privilege is now used to keep information from congressional investigators, this was not always the case and is not supported by legal precedent. Richard Nixon sought to protect himself from a congressional investigation, but the Supreme Court decided that Congress may request relevant information from the executive branch, action which led to Nixon's resignation on August 9, 1974, in the largest political scandal in U.S. history up to that time.

In evaluating President George W. Bush's latest outlandish invocation of executive privilege, through White House counsel Fred Fielding, to stonewall Congress over the firings of nine U.S. attorneys, turn your memory clock back approximately 35 years to the spring of 1973.

The nation was transfixed by the testimony of John Dean, former White House counsel, before the Senate Watergate

Bruce Fein, "Executive Nonsense," Slate.com, July 11, 2007. www.slate.com/id/2170247/entry/2137335/nav/ais. Copyright © 2007 Washington Post, Newsweek. Distributed by United Feature Syndicate, Inc.

committee. He meticulously recounted presidential conversations in the Oval Office that implicated both himself and President Richard M. Nixon in obstruction of justice. Mr. Dean's unbosoming of presidential communications led to the voting of three articles of impeachment against Mr. Nixon by the House judiciary committee and the president's subsequent resignation on Aug. 9, 1974. President Nixon never sought to silence Dean by claiming a constitutional privilege to keep confidential presidential communications, which Congress sought in exercising its authority to investigate crime or maladministration in the executive branch. Remember, of course, that Nixon was not bashful about asserting monarchlike powers. He attempted to prevent special prosecutor Leon Jaworski from accessing presidential tapes and documents, a stance rejected by the Supreme Court in *United States v. Nixon*. He also barked at newscaster David Frost in a postresignation interview that anything the president does is legal.

Executive privilege is a concoction, then, to protect secrecy for the sake of secret government.

Mr. Fielding served as Dean's deputy. He has never maintained that President Nixon could have muzzled Dean by invoking executive privilege. But that is the inescapable implication of his defense of President Bush's prerogative to silence former presidential aides Sara M. Taylor and Harriet E. Miers, whom Congress has subpoenaed, and to shield presidential documents that have also been subpoenaed. Fielding elaborated his reasons in a July 9, 2007, letter to the chairmen of the House and Senate judiciary committees. If his unconvincing rationale is accepted, the congressional power to check executive-branch lawlessness or maladministration will be crippled. A second edition of Watergate could go undetected.

Sunshine Is the Best Disinfectant

Justice requires the appearance of justice. To command public confidence, the Justice Department—yes, like Caesar's wife— must be above suspicion. But suspicion has arisen that the White House intended to manipulate U.S. attorneys in some instances to harass Democrats with contrived voting fraud prosecutions or otherwise. The committees' interest in exposing misuse of the president's power to appoint and remove executive officials is compelling. As Justice Louis Brandeis observed, sunshine is the best disinfectant. The congressional judiciary committees are further legitimately investigating whether Attorney General Alberto Gonzales or other Department of Justice officials committed perjury or endeavored to obstruct Congress' investigation by misrepresenting White House involvement in the decisions to remove the U.S. attorneys. The Supreme Court, in the 1957 case *Watkins v. United States*, explained that Congress enjoys the power to "inquire into and publicize corruption, maladministration, or inefficiencies" in the executive branch, including crimes. President Bush's assertion of executive privilege to stymie the committees' well-founded investigations is wildly misplaced.

The president's claim of privilege pivots on a false assumption wrongly endorsed by the Supreme Court in *Nixon v. United States*: namely, that the president will not receive candid and unfettered advice from subordinates absent a guarantee that their communications will remain confidential. What nonsense. I have worked in and out of government for 38 years. I have never heard any high or low executive-branch official so much as insinuate that presidential advice had been or might be skewed or withheld if confidentiality were not guaranteed. The gravity of advising the president universally overcomes anxieties over possible embarrassment through subsequent publicity. Moreover, every presidential adviser knows that confidentiality is never ironclad. Presidents routinely waive executive privilege in jockeying with Congress;

confidentiality is always subservient to a criminal investigation or prosecution under the Nixon precedent; and leaks to the media of confidential presidential memos or conversations overflow like the Nile. Indeed, President Bush has himself waived the privilege repeatedly in the ongoing U.S. attorneys investigations by the two committees.

Executive privilege is a concoction, then, to protect secrecy for the sake of secret government, while transparency is the rule of enlightened democracies to ensure political account-ability and to deter folly or wrongdoing. Still, let's assume for a moment that executive privilege is in fact needed to pro-mote presidential candor. The privilege still would not justify silencing presidential aides like Ms. Taylor or John Dean, who are eager to disclose their communications. Candor is not threatened by a rule that entitles each presidential communi-cant to decide for him- or herself whether to speak publicly or not.

What Happens When the President Is Wrong?

President Bush insists that Congress has no business snooping into the firings of the U.S. attorneys, because his constitu-tional power to remove them is absolute. He cites the 1926 case *Myers v. United States*. The president is wrong. A removal motivated by race or religion would be unconstitutional. Fur-ther, Congress has a legitimate interest in airing the facts un-derlying executive discretion to inform the public so that citi-zens can adjust their political or voting loyalties accordingly. The Constitution's separation of powers is implicated only when one branch seeks to exercise a "controlling influence" over the powers of another. Congress does not dominate the president's authority to remove U.S. attorneys by exposing reasons for his decisions that may be indicative of a scheme to manipulate law enforcement personnel for partisan political advantage. Even if Congress cannot legislate against such removals, it can deter them by public embarrassment.

Moreover, the committees are also keenly interested to learn if Attorney General Gonzales or his aides committed perjury or corruptly endeavored to obstruct a congressional investigation into minimizing the White House role in the firings. No Department of Justice official has claimed responsibility for listing the U.S. attorneys to be fired. That points the arrow of likely culpability at the White House, contrary to Gonzales' averments. The testimonies of Taylor and Miers are critical to getting at the truth of White House involvement and to Gonzales' vulnerability to prosecution or impeachment. The Bush administration itself cannot be trusted with the truth-finding task because of the conflict of interest.

President Bush errantly claims that Congress must prove that presidential communications are "demonstrably critical" to its oversight functions to trump executive privilege. In the Nixon case, however, the Supreme Court did not require the special prosecutor to establish that the presidential tapes and documents at issue were "demonstrably critical" to winning convictions. Relevance was sufficient. The standard for Congress should be no different when criminality or maladministration is under investigation. Unless it is examined, there is no way to know whether a piece of evidence is the proverbial smoking gun, akin to Dean's testimony against Nixon. If Congress knew in advance that the information it seeks was vital, no further investigation would be needed.

In sum, Congress should win any court clash over President Bush's assertion of executive privilege over the firings of the U.S. attorneys. Litigation, however, is lead-footed. Victory delayed to the committees may be victory denied because it is victory delayed. Congress needs to adjust and accelerate the current mechanisms for challenging executive privilege. But that is a subject for another day.

Organizations to Contact

The editors have compiled the following list of organizations concerned with the issues debated in this book. The descriptions are derived from materials provided by the organizations. All have publications or information available for interested readers. The list was compiled on the date of publication of the present volume; the information provided here may change. Be aware that many organizations take several weeks or longer to respond to inquiries, so allow as much time as possible.

American Civil Liberties Union (ACLU)
125 Broad St., 18th Floor, New York, NY   10004
(212) 549-2500 • fax: (212) 549-2646
Web site: www.aclu.org

The ACLU is a national organization that works to defend Americans' civil rights as guaranteed by the U.S. Constitution. It opposes limits on political campaign contributions on the grounds that such restrictions violate the First Amendment, and it is a watchdog for political scandals on the grounds that they interfere with democracy and the rights of the American people.

**American Enterprise Institute
for Public Policy Research (AEI)**
1150 17th St. NW, Washington, DC   20036
(202) 862-5800 • fax: (202) 862-7177
e-mail: Laura.Drinkwine@aei.org
Web site: www.aei.org

AEI is a conservative think tank that studies such issues as government regulation, religion, philosophy, and legal policy.

American League of Lobbyists (ALL)
P.O. Box 30005, Alexandria, VA   22310
(703) 960-3011

e-mail: alldc.org@erols.com
Web site: www.alldc.org

Established in 1979 as a nonprofit organization, the American League of Lobbyists (ALL) is the national professional association dedicated exclusively to lobbying. ALL's mission is to enhance the development of professionalism, competence, and high ethical standards for advocates in the public policy arena, and to collectively address challenges affecting the first amendment right to "petition the government for redress of grievances." ALL actively encourages the advancement of ethical lobbying practices.

Brookings Institution
1775 Massachusetts Ave. NW, Washington, DC   20036
(202) 797-6000 • fax: (202) 797-6004
Web site: www.brook.edu

Founded in 1927, the institution is a liberal research and education organization that publishes material on economics, government, and foreign policy. It strives to serve as a bridge between scholarship and public policy, bringing new knowledge to the attention of decision makers and providing scholars with improved insight into public policy issues. Its publications include the quarterly *Brookings Review* and *Campaign Finance Reform: A Sourcebook*.

Cato Institute
1000 Massachusetts Ave. NW, Washington, DC   20001-5403
(202) 842-0200 • fax: (202) 842-3490
e-mail: cato@cato.org
Web site: www.cato.org

The Cato Institute is a libertarian public policy research foundation dedicated to limiting the control of government and protecting individual liberties. It offers numerous publications on public policy issues, including the triennial *Cato Journal*, the bimonthly newsletter *Cato Policy Report*, and the quarterly magazine *Regulation*.

Center for Public Integrity (CPI)
910 Seventeenth St. NW, 7th Floor, Washington, DC 20006
(202) 466-1300 • fax: (202) 466-1101
e-mail: scarpinelli@publicintegrity.org
Web site: www.publicintegrity.org

The center is a nonprofit organization that examines ethics-related issues in government. Its mission is to produce original investigative journalism to make institutional power more transparent and accountable. The center publishes numerous studies, reports, and newsletters on political scandals.

Center for Responsive Politics (CRP)
1101 Fourteenth St., NW, Suite 1030
Washington, DC 20005-5635
(202) 857-0044 • fax (202) 857-7809
e-mail: info@crp.org
Web site: www.opensecrets.org

The Center for Responsive Politics is a nonpartisan, nonprofit research group based in Washington, DC that tracks money in politics and its effect on elections and public policy. The center conducts research on campaign finance issues for the news media, academics, activists, and the public at large. The center's work is aimed at creating more educated voters, an involved citizenry, and a more responsive government. It publishes the *Capital Eye* newsletter and numerous reports.

Century Foundation
41 E. 70th St., New York, NY 10021
(212) 535-4441 • fax: (212) 879-9197
e-mail: info@tcf.org
Web site: www.tcf.org

This research foundation, formerly known as the Twentieth-Century Fund, sponsors analysis of economic policy, foreign affairs, and domestic political issues. It publishes numerous books, reports, and articles, many of which focus on political scandals. It also hosts project sites, including Liberty Under Attack and Reform Elections.org.

Christian Coalition (CC)

P.O. Box 37030, Washington, DC   20013-7030 USA
(202) 479-6900 • fax: (202) 479-4260
e-mail: coalition@cc.org
Web site: www.cc.org

Founded by evangelist Pat Robertson, the coalition is a grass-roots political organization of Christian fundamentalists working to elect moral legislators and stop what it believes is the moral decay of government. Its publications include the monthly newsletter *The Religious Right Watch* and the monthly tabloid *Christian American*.

Common Cause

1250 Connecticut Ave. NW, Suite 600
Washington, DC   20036
(202) 833-1200
Web site: www.commoncause.org

Common Cause is a liberal lobbying organization that works to improve the ethical standards of Congress and government in general. Its priorities include campaign finance reform, making government officials accountable for their actions, and promoting civil rights for all citizens. Common Cause publishes the quarterly *Common Cause Magazine* as well as position papers and reports.

Council for Excellence in Government

1301 K Street NW, Suite 450 West, Washington, DC   20005
(202) 728-0418 • fax: (202) 728-0422
e-mail: ceg@excelgov.org
Web site: www.excelgov.org

The Council for Excellence in Government works to improve the performance of government at all levels and government's place in the lives and esteem of American citizens. The council seeks to create stronger public-sector leadership and management, driven by innovation and focused on results and increased citizen confidence and participation in government, through better understanding of government and its role. Its publications include *A Survivor's Guide for Government Executives* and *The Prune Book: The 45 Toughest Financial Management Jobs in Washington.*

Democratic National Committee (DNC)
430 S. Capitol St. SE, Washington, DC   20003
(202) 863-8000
Web site: www.democrats.org

The DNC formulates and promotes policies and positions of the Democratic Party. Its Web site includes information on party activities and campaigns.

Federal Election Commission (FEC)
999 E St. NW, Washington, DC   20463
(800) 424 9530
Web site: www.fec.gov

The FEC is an independent regulatory agency created by Congress in 1975 to administer the Federal Election Campaign Act (FECA). It oversees public funding of presidential elections and enforces campaign finance laws. Its Web site includes financial disclosure reports and data about national election campaigns.

Institute for Philosophy and Public Policy (IPPP)
University of Maryland, College Park, MD   20742
(301) 405-4753 • fax: (301) 314-9346
Web site: www.puaf.umd.edu/IPPP

IPPP investigates the conceptual and ethical aspects of public policy formulation and debate. It seeks to develop curricula that will bring philosophical issues before future policymakers and citizens. The institute publishes the quarterlies *Philosophy and Public Policy* and *Report from the Institute for Philosophy and Public Policy.*

Judicial Watch

P.O. Box 44444, Washington, DC   20026
(888) 593-8442 • fax: (202) 646-5199
e-mail: info@judicialwatch.org
Web site: www.judicialwatch.org

Judicial Watch is a nonpartisan conservative foundation meant to serve as a watchdog against corrupt practices and ethical and legal transgressions in the federal government. It brought several lawsuits against the Clinton administration for what it considered to be scandalous acts of misconduct and betrayal of the public trust, including illegal campaign fundraising. Its Web site provides information about the cases in which the organization is involved. Among its many publications is the periodical *The Verdict.*

League of Women Voters

1730 M St. NW, Suite 1000, Washington, DC   20036-4508
(202) 429-1965 • fax: (202) 429-0854
Web site: www.lwv.org

The League of Women Voters is a private nonpartisan political organization that works to encourage an informed and active participation of citizens in government. It provides informational materials and position papers on voter participation and campaign finance on its Web site.

Public Campaign

1320 19th St., NW, Suite M-1, Washington, DC   20036
(202) 293-0222 • fax: (202) 293-0202
e-mail: info@pcactionfund.org
Web site: www.publiccampaign.org

Public Campaign is a nonpartisan campaign finance reform organization that seeks to reduce the role of special interest money in U.S. politics. It publishes educational materials on various campaign reform measures and provides news, polling data, and commentary on money in politics on its Web site.

Public Citizen
1600 20th St. NW, Washington, DC   20009-1001
(202) 588-1000 • fax: (202) 588-7799
Web site: www.citizen.org

Founded by Ralph Nader, Public Citizen is a nonpartisan organization that promotes government and corporate accountability, consumer rights in the marketplace, and safe products through lobbying, research, public outreach, and litigation. It publishes the bimonthly magazine *Public Citizen* and numerous other publications and reports.

Republican National Committee (RNC)
310 First St. SE, Washington, DC   20003
(202) 863-8500 • fax: (202) 863-8820
e-mail: info@rnc.org
Web site: www.rnc.org

The RNC formulates and promotes policies and positions of the Republican Party. Its Web site offers information on party activities and campaigns.

U.S. Term Limits
1511 K St. NW, Suite 540, Washington, DC   20005
(202) 393-6440 • fax: (202) 393-6434
Web site: www.ustl.org

U.S. Term Limits is a nonprofit, nonpartisan organization chartered to restore citizen control of government by rallying Americans to limit legislators' congressional and state and local government terms of office. It publishes a number of papers as part of its Term Limit Outlook Series and the monthly newsletter *No Uncertain Terms.*

Bibliography

Books

Lanny Davis   *Scandal: How "Gotcha" Politics Is Destroying America*. Basingstoke, Hampshire, U.K.: Palgrave Macmillan, August 2007.

John W. Dean   *Worse than Watergate: The Secret Presidency of George W. Bush*. Boston: Little, Brown, 2004.

Mark Grossman   *Political Corruption in America: An Encyclopedia of Scandals, Power, and Greed*. Oxford, U.K.: ABC-Clio, 2003.

Michael A. Ledeen   Machiavelli on Modern Leadership: Why Machiavelli's Iron Rules Are as Timely and Important Today as Five Centuries Ago. New York: Truman Talley Books, 2007.

Kim Long   *The Almanac of Political Corruption, Scandals & Dirty Politics*. New York: Delacorte Press, 2007.

Frank Rich   *The Greatest Story Ever Sold: The Decline and Fall of Truth from 9/11 to Katrina*. New York: Penguin Press, 2006.

Larry J. Sabato, Mark Stencel, and S. Robert Lichter   *Peepshow: Media and Politics in an Age of Scandal*. Lanham, MD: Rowman & Littlefield, 2001.

John B. Thomson *Political Scandal: Power and Visibility in the Media Age.* Cambridge, U.K.: Polity Press, 2000.

Juliet Williams, George Shulman, Jeremy Varon, and Joshua Gamson *Public Affairs: Politics in the Age of Sex Scandals.* Durham, NC: Duke University Press, 2004.

Bob Woodward and Carl Bernstein *All the President's Men.* New York: Pocket, 1974.

Periodicals

Jimmy Carter "We Need Fewer Secrets." *Washington Post,* July 3, 2006.

David Corn "Enron End Run." *Nation,* February 18, 2002.

Michael Isikoff and Evan Thomas "Follow the Yellowcake Road," *Newsweek,* July 28, 2003.

Leslie Lenkowsky "How Washington's Political Scandals Could Harm Nonprofit Groups," *Chronicle of Philanthropy,* June 23, 2005.

Mark Levinson "Business Scandals and Democracy," *Dissent,* Fall 2002.

Robert MacDermid "Buying Back Our Political Parties," *Canadian Dimension,* November 2000.

Warren Mass "Lessons from Haditha," *New American,* July 10, 2006.

Stryker McGuire   "I Did It My Way," *Newsweek*, February 26, 2007.

David W. Moore   "Little Political Fallout from Business Scandals," *Gallup Poll Tuesday Briefing*, July 2002.

Jonathan S. Morris and Rosalee A. Clawson   "Media Coverage of Congress in the 1990s: Scandals, Personalities, and the Prevalence of Policy and Process," *Political Communication*, July–September, 2005.

William Powers   "The Scandal Factory," *Atlantic*, October 10, 2006.

Frank Rich   "I Did Have Sexual Relations with That Woman," *New York Times*, July 22, 2007.

David Roth   "What Congress Doesn't Know Will Hurt You," *Fortune*, August 12, 2002.

Marc Schmitt   "The Limits of Limits," *American Prospect*, March 2006.

William Schneider   "K Street's Capitol Connection," *Atlantic*, January 24, 2006.

Siobhan Smith   "For Political Scandals, Timing Is Everything: Sex Scandals Are Always Hard Stories, but Pending Elections Add an Extra Ethical Wrinkle." *Quill*, April 2005.

Cass R. Sunstein   "Defining Executive Privilege," *Boston Globe*, July 12, 2007.

Kenneth T. Walsh "Springtime, and the Smell of Scandal," *U.S. News & World Report*, April 2000.

Internet Sources

Eric Alterman, "Think Again: The Pure Politics of 'Privilege,'" Center for American Progress, July 12, 2007. www.americanprogress.org/issues/2007/07/alterman_privilege.html.

Angela Coleman, "Mark Foley and Other U.S. Political Scandals: Why Are We So Surprised?" Associated Content, October 18, 2006. www.associatedcontent.com/article/71891/mark_foley_and_other_us_political_sca ndals.html.

Joel Connelly, "Political Scandals Thick as Trees in Alaska," Seattlepi.com, July 29, 2007. http://seattlepi.nwsource.com/connelly/325567_joel30.html.

Robert J. Elisberg, "Horrors! The Political Scandal of All Political Scandals," Huffington Post.com, July 10, 2007. www.huffingtonpost.com/robert-j-elisberg/horrors-the-political-s_b_55614.html.

Bruce Fein, "Executive Nonsense: Bush's Assertion of Privilege Is Wildly Misplaced—and Could Lead to Another Watergate," Slate.com, July 11, 2007. www.slate.com/id/2170247/entry/2137335/nav/ais/.

David Paul Kuhn and John F. Harris, "GOP Fears for Credibility after Scandals," The Politico, July 11, 2007. www.politico.com/news/stories/0707/4873.html.

Norman J. Ornstein, "'Executive Privilege' Has Storied History, but It Can Be Abused," American Enterprise Institute for Public Policy, July 11, 2007. www.aei.org/publications/filter.all,pubID.26472/pub_detail.asp.

Index